Ordnance

Northumbria
Walks

Pathfinder Guide
Compiled by John Brooks   Series editor: Brian Conduit

Key to colour coding

The walks are divided into three broad categories, indicated by the following colours:

Short, easy walks

Walks of moderate length, likely to involve some modest uphill walking

More challenging walks, which may be longer and/or over more rugged terrain, often with some stiff climbs

Acknowledgements

We would like to thank Mike Ogden and Simon Hodgson of Durham County Council Environment Department for their help in preparing the text and maps, and Peter Howe of the National Park and Countryside Department, Northumberland County Council for his help in checking the rights of way.

While every care has been taken to ensure the accuracy of the route directions, the publishers cannot accept responsibility for errors or omissions, or for changes in details given. It has to be emphasised that the countryside is not static: hedges and fences can be removed, field boundaries can alter, footpaths can be rerouted and changes of ownership can result in the closure or diversion of some concessionary paths. Also paths that are easy and pleasant for walking in fine conditions may become slippery, muddy and difficult in wet weather and stepping stones over rivers and streams may become impassable.

Ordnance Survey   ISBN 0-319-00214-4
Jarrold Publishing   ISBN 0-7117-0552-6

First published 1991 by Ordnance Survey and Jarrold Publishing
Reprinted 1994

Ordnance Survey
Romsey Road
Maybush
Southampton SO9 4DH

Jarrold Publishing
Whitefriars
Norwich NR3 1TR

© Crown copyright 1991

Printed in Great Britain by Jarrold Printing, Norwich. 2/94

Previous page: *the Meeting of the Waters, Teesdale*

Contents

Introduction to Northumbria

Northumbria was the northernmost kingdom of Anglo-Saxon England, embracing the land north of the Humber. Some years ago the name was claimed by the tourist board promoting north-eastern England who used it to describe the modern counties of Northumberland, Durham, Tyne and Wear, and Cleveland. Although there are many footpaths to be found in the latter two counties, most walkers will realise that for them Northumbria means Northumberland and the upland parts of County Durham.

It is only recently that this region has been 'discovered' by the tourist. As anyone knows who has left booking holiday accommodation to the last moment, Northumbria is now a boom area. The reasons for this sudden popularity are easy to understand. In the case of Northumberland, the county has a long, and never overcrowded, shoreline of sandy beaches interspersed with rocky coves and beautiful estuaries. The same coastline provides excellent links for golfers and its springy turf also serves walkers well. In the pastoral plain which lies beyond there are a handful of interesting and historic market towns. In the same way County Durham has its grand cathedral city as the hub of a farming hinterland.

To the west are the highlands. In the south these belong to the Pennines — beautiful, sparsely populated moorlands penetrated by the headwaters of the great rivers: the Tees, Wear, and Tyne. Further to the north the hills are the Cheviots, where the tops (and the valleys too) are even more lonely than those further south. Here there are many routes where on most days you can walk for hours (or even all day) without meeting a soul. Your senses will be assaulted by the sound of

Cup-and-ring patterns

silence, very disconcerting if you are not used to it. The pounding of blood through the body as one struggles up the flanks of, say, The Cheviot can be quite unnerving. It underlines the need to take care in this countryside, especially if you are walking on your own.

To many people perhaps more used to the crowded popular routes of the Peaks or Lakes this will be the main appeal of Northumbria. Yet there are other unique attractions. The region is well steeped in history, both secular and religious. Before the beginnings of recorded history man left his mark on the landscape — witness the mysterious cup-and-ring patterns carved on boulders which stand in remote positions on many of the moors. Northumberland's most famous monument belongs to the military ascendancy established here by Emperor Hadrian in the early years of the second century. His magnificent wall, which once strode across northern England from coast to coast, is the landscape feature which lingers longest in visitors' memories. As the most picturesque part of its course follows a crag rising high above the surrounding moorland, a walk along its snaking course must be included amongst the most spectacular of British walks.

Later monuments to military ascendancy include the castles and towers of the Middle Ages built, like the wall, to check the rampaging tribes of Caledonia (though to be fair, their southern neighbours did their share of pillaging too). Many of the mansions of the region incorporate medieval towers in their structure, though the more famous strongholds — Alnwick, Raby, Warkworth, Barnard Castle, Dunstanburgh — remain much as they were built (albeit that the latter three are ruinous) and convey the same message to any intending aggressor today.

Northumbria continues to have strong links with the military: the Ministry of Defence owns twenty per cent of the land within the National Park, most of it to the south of the Coquet Valley. This land is used as a Dry Training Area, i.e. no live ammunition is fired there. However there is live firing in the other extensive training grounds which lie outside the boundaries of the National Park.

Industrial history has also left its mark on the region. Unhappily, much landscape remains scarred by the extraction of coal, lead, roadstone and other minerals. This hidden wealth brought prosperity to landowners in the eighteenth and nineteenth centuries, though not necessarily to the workmen who toiled to bring the minerals to the surface. The moors of County Durham are littered with the remains of lead and barytes mines abandoned in the nineteenth century. Though they lack the engine houses

Hadrian's Wall from Hotbank Crags

which bestow romance on the disused mines of Cornwall, their crumbling buildings set amidst desolate hills bring drama to the lonely landscape. The disused railways which once served them often provide walkers with interesting highland routes.

In 1956 the Northumberland National Park was created to maintain the unique character of upland Northumberland. Its 396 square miles (1,026 square km) fall within two distinct conjoined areas — firstly the Cheviots and then the district surrounding Hadrian's Wall. Although its area may be small compared with other national parks and it does not yet attract as many visitors, Northumberland manages to present a caring and helpful face to those who use its facilities. Most of the popular beauty spots have maps detailing the rights of way and permissive paths of the district. These are generally well waymarked.

The National Trust also has extensive interests in the region. They own stately properties such as Wallington Hall and Cragside (which has 40 miles (64 km) of footpaths and carriage drives) and other unexpected parcels of land. Some, like their Dunstanburgh Castle and Hadrian's Wall estates for example, are administered by English Heritage. The latter demesne covers 2,000 acres (809 ha), including 4½ miles (7.25 km) of the most spectacular part of the wall itself.

Allen Banks, at the confluence of the rivers Tyne and Allen, is a beautiful woodland property where visitors can roam for hours over hill and dale and enjoy wide vistas as well as more enclosed beauty spots by riverside or tarn. Much of the coast of the northern part of Northumberland is National Trust property as is one of the region's most famous viewpoints — Penshaw Hill in Tyne and Wear — which affords tremendous views from the south of Northumbria to the far north. It was supposed to be the resting-place of the Lambton Worm, a serpent which terrorised the district in the Middle Ages.

The making of the landscape

Ice, fire and water all had a hand in creating the landscape of Northumbria. The Cheviot massif was formed 380 million years ago when molten volcanic rock was forced to the surface through layers of sandstone to cover an area of 350 square miles (906 square km). These flows of lava form a very hard rock called andesite which supports moor mat grass or nadus rather than heather. This grass is bleached white in summer and is seldom eaten by sheep. From this comes the sobriquet for the Cheviot uplands: the White Land. All this may amaze some walkers in the district who remember best their arduous struggles through virtually impenetrable heather. Nadus flourishes in the less well drained land on the tops while heather, with bracken, likes the drier soil of the middle slopes. Northumberland's most famous roadstone, from Biddlestone Quarry, is slightly different in composition to andesite though formed in the same way. The pink rock (felsite) is used to surface a famous royal driveway — the Mall in London — as well as the hard shoulders of motorways.

Further igneous intrusions followed the outpouring of the lava through the sandstone. These formed the granite domes of The Cheviot and Hedgehope and, where they came into contact with andesite, resulted in the even harder granite which is weathered into Dartmoor-like tors such as Housey Crag and Long Crag on the south side of Harthope Valley.

After the drama of all this volcanic activity came aeons of comparative tranquillity during which deep layers of sediment were laid down around the Cheviot massif. This sandstone was later uplifted to form the Simonside Hills.

The Carboniferous era affected the Pennine uplands rather than the Cheviots. Limestone and millstone grit were deposited in Yorkshire, Derbyshire and Durham. However, at the end of the era tremendous earth movements took place which uplifted the Cheviots and tilted them eastwards. At the same time faults appeared radiating from the hub of the massif, the displacement of strata resulting in great cracks in the surface − from which the Breamish, College and Harthope valleys derive. This activity generated more volcanic intrusions, and it was at this time, 295 million years ago, that Northumberland's most celebrated geological feature came into existence − the Whin Sill.

This event has been graphically compared to hot jam being squeezed between the layers of a sandwich cake. It should be added that it was also like a child's efforts in this direction. The lava squirted out everywhere. To the east it resulted in the formation of the Farne Islands as well as the great crags on which the castles of Dunstanburgh and Bamburgh are sited. Further south it intruded into layers of carboniferous limestone which were subsequently eroded to leave the Sill as an upstanding ridge snaking across country, the steep scarp facing north, which proved convenient for the Romans.

Northumbria escaped the more violent events of later geological periods and it was not until the Ice Age (two million years ago) that further significant events took place which altered the face of the land. Although the main river valleys of the region had already been etched before this climatic change, the great weight of ice and the debris carried down carved them into their distinctive U-shapes. The spoil eroded from the land mass, which was eventually dumped all over the region, did not just derive from the Cheviots. Some came from as far away as Galloway. The most significant result of glaciation was the making of a fertile coastal plain from the boulder clay deposited after the ice began to retreat, about 17,000 years ago. Glaciation can also be blamed for the treacherous scree slopes which are so hated by walkers and scramblers. After the ice

A Cheviot adder

melted, the mountains, relieved of its weight, were slightly raised up. This allowed streams to scour out their valleys more vigorously than hitherto, resulting in deeply etched gorges.

Practical walking in Northumbria

There can be no doubt that the hills and mountains of the region can sometimes become one of the most hostile and potentially lethal environments to be found in Britain. At a distance the mountains look innocuous, gently curved monsters lying on the horizon, perhaps drenched in golden evening sunlight. Do not be charmed by this disguise: like all regions of highland, they possess a multitude of dangers for the unwary.

Two of the hazards go hand in hand − navigation and weather. Many of the routes written up for this book are across lonely tracts of countryside where you are unlikely to encounter any other walkers. Although footpaths are clearly marked on the map, they may not be obvious on the ground. For this reason you will need a good compass, and for the more demanding routes you should also take a copy of the relevant Pathfinder map. It is very easy to drift off the perimeter of the map extracts printed here, and often the reference points for your bearings will be outside the area shown. A particular difficulty in Northumbria is that it is hard to find a suitable landmark to direct the compass towards. In Wales or the Lake District the peaks are usually very distinctive: here they tend to be anonymous shapes, rather like whales resting on the skyline.

Taking bearings needs good visibility, and the Cheviots are particularly notorious for the way in which cloud can suddenly descend to wrap you in a cocoon of isolation. Fortunately there are not too many precipices to drop off, but being lost here can be a frightening experience, and you cannot rely on other more experienced walkers discovering you by accident as might happen in the Pennines or the Lakes. Thus a favourable weather forecast is essential. Loss of visibility can herald other changes in the weather. The combination of wind and heavy rain is potentially dangerous; don't forget that a strong headwind along the ridges can mean that extra time may be needed for a walk, so listen to the forecast and note the wind's direction and strength and make due allowance.

Winter, of course, brings extra danger and it would be foolish to undertake the longer walks in this book then unless you are very experienced. Even so it would still be foolhardy to attempt them alone. If you do go off walking on your own, at any season, be sure to leave details of your route with someone responsible. Read the section on 'Safety on the hills' (inside back cover) and be sure to wear suitable clothing and footwear and to take spare clothing, food, drink, a torch, first-aid kit and whistle.

Keep a good lookout for adders on lower paths; they are surprisingly common and may be torpid in the spring on emerging from hibernation. A last hazard raises its head in late summer when the grouse shooters descend on the moors (this in a literal sense these days when parties are flown in by helicopter). Walkers are obviously unwelcome on footpaths when there is shooting from butts nearby, but on well organised grouse moors local tourist offices are warned of impending shoots. It is certainly worth checking before venturing on routes such as that across Rake Gill (Walk 27) which go close to the butts.

The National Parks and countryside recreation

Ten National Parks were created in England and Wales as a result of an Act of Parliament in 1949, and an eleventh was established under special legislation in 1989. In addition to these, there are numerous specially designated Areas of Outstanding Natural Beauty, Country and Regional Parks, Sites of Special Scientific Interest and picnic areas scattered throughout England, Wales and Scotland, all of which share the twin aims of preservation of the countryside and public accessibility and enjoyment.

In trying to define a National Park, one point to bear in mind is that unlike many overseas ones, Britain's National Parks are not owned by the nation. The vast bulk of the land in them is under private ownership. John Dower, whose report in 1945 created

their framework, defined a National Park as 'an extensive area of beautiful and relatively wild country in which, for the nation's benefit and by appropriate national decision and action, (a) the characteristic landscape beauty is strictly preserved, (b) access and facilities for public open-air enjoyment are amply provided, (c) wildlife and buildings and places of architectural and historic interest are suitably protected, while (d) established farming use is effectively maintained'.

The concept of having designated areas of protected countryside grew out of a number of factors that appeared towards the end of the nineteenth century; principally greater facilities and opportunities for travel, the development of various conservationist bodies and the establishment of National Parks abroad. Apart from a few of the early individual travellers such as Celia Fiennes and Daniel Defoe, who were usually more concerned with commenting on agricultural improvements, the appearance of towns and the extent of antiquities to be found than with the wonders of nature, interest in the countryside as a source of beauty, spiritual refreshment and recreation, and, along with that, an interest in conserving it, did not arise until the Victorian era. Towards the end of the eighteenth century, improvements in road transport enabled the wealthy to visit regions that had hitherto been largely inaccessible and, by the middle of the nineteenth century, the construction of the railways opened up such possibilities to the middle classes and, later on, to the working classes in even greater numbers. At the same time, the Romantic movement was in full swing and, encouraged by the works of Wordsworth, Coleridge and Shelley, interest and enthusiasm for wild places, including the mountain, moorland and hill regions of northern and western Britain, were now in vogue. Eighteenth-century taste had thought of the Scottish Highlands, the Lake District and Snowdonia as places to avoid, preferring controlled order and symmetry in nature as well as in architecture and town planning. But upper and middle class Victorian travellers were thrilled and awed by what they saw as the untamed savagery and wilderness of mountain peaks, deep and secluded gorges, thundering waterfalls, towering cliffs and rocky crags. In addition, there was a growing reaction against the materialism and squalor of Victorian industrialisation and urbanisation and a desire to escape from the formality and artificiality of town life into areas of unspoilt natural beauty.

A result of this was the formation of a number of different societies, all concerned with the 'great outdoors': naturalist groups, rambling clubs and conservationist

Dunstanburgh Castle

organisations. One of the earliest of these was the Commons, Open Spaces and Footpaths Preservation Society, originally founded in 1865 to preserve commons and develop public access to the countryside. Particularly influential was the National Trust, set up in 1895 to protect and maintain both places of natural beauty and places of historic interest, and, later on, the Councils for the Preservation of Rural England, Wales and Scotland, three separate bodies that came into being between 1926 and 1928.

The world's first National Park was the Yellowstone Park in the United States, designated in 1872. This was followed by others in Canada, South Africa, Germany, Switzerland, New Zealand and elsewhere, but in Britain such places did not come about until after the Second World War. Proposals for the creation of areas of protected countryside were made before the First World War and during the 1920s and 1930s, but nothing was done. The growing demand from people in towns for access to open country and the reluctance of landowners – particularly those who owned large expanses of uncultivated moorland – to grant it led to a number of ugly incidents, in particular the mass trespass in the Peak District in 1932, when fighting took place between ramblers and gamekeepers and some of the trespassers received stiff prison sentences.

It was in the climate exemplified by the Beveridge Report and the subsequent creation of the welfare state, however, that calls for countryside conservation and access came to fruition in parliament. Based on the recommendations of the Dower Report (1945) and the Hobhouse Committee (1947), the National Parks and Countryside Act of 1949 provided for the designation and preservation of areas both of great scenic beauty and of particular wildlife and scientific interest throughout Britain. More specifically it provided for the creation of National Parks in England and Wales. Scotland was excluded because, with greater areas of open space and a smaller population, there were fewer pressures on the Scottish countryside and therefore there was felt to be less need for the creation of such protected areas.

A National Parks Commission was set up, and over the next eight years ten areas were designated as parks; seven in England (Northumberland, Lake District, North York Moors, Yorkshire Dales, Peak District, Exmoor and Dartmoor) and three in Wales (Snowdonia, Brecon Beacons and Pembrokeshire Coast). At the same time the Commission was also given the responsibility for designating other smaller areas of high recreational and scenic qualities (Areas of Outstanding Natural Beauty), plus the power to propose and develop long-distance footpaths, now called National Trails, though it was not until 1965 that the first of these, the Pennine Way, came into existence.

Further changes came with the Countryside Act of 1968 (a similar one for Scotland had been passed in 1967). The National Parks Commission was replaced by the Countryside Commission, which was now to oversee and review virtually all aspects of countryside conservation, access and provision of recreational amenities. The Country Parks, which were smaller areas of countryside often close to urban areas, came into being. A number of long-distance footpaths were created, followed by an even greater number of unofficial long- or middle-distance paths, devised by individuals, ramblers' groups or local authorities. Provision of car parks and visitor centres, waymarking of public rights of way and the production of leaflets giving suggestions for walking routes all increased, a reflection both of increased leisure and of a greater desire for recreational activity, of which walking in particular, now recognised as the most popular leisure pursuit, has had a great explosion of interest.

In 1989 the Norfolk and Suffolk Broads joined the National Park family, special legislation being passed to cover the area's navigational interests as well as aspects of conservation and public enjoyment.

The authorities who administer the individual National Parks have the very difficult task of reconciling the interests of the people who live and earn their living within them with those of the visitors. National Parks, and the other designated areas, are not living museums. Developments of various kinds, in housing, transport and rural industries, are needed. There is pressure to exploit the resources of the area, through more intensive farming, or through increased quarrying and forestry, extraction of minerals or the construction of reservoirs.

In the end it all comes down to a question of balance; a balance between conservation and 'sensitive development'. On the one hand there is a responsibility to preserve and enhance the natural beauty of the National Parks and to promote their enjoyment by the public, and on the other, the needs and well-being of the people living and working in them have to be borne in mind.

The National Trust

Anyone who likes visiting places of natural beauty and/or historic interest has cause to be grateful to the National Trust. Without it, many such places would probably have vanished by now, either under an avalanche of concrete and bricks and mortar or through reservoir construction or blanket afforestation.

It was in response to the pressures on the countryside posed by the relentless march of Victorian industrialisation that the Trust was set up in 1895. Its founders, inspired by the common goals of protecting and conserving Britain's national heritage and widening public access to it, were Sir Robert Hunter, Octavia Hill and Canon Rawnsley; a solicitor, a social reformer and a clergyman respectively. The latter was particularly influential. As a canon of Carlisle Cathedral and vicar of Crosthwaite (near Keswick), he was concerned about threats to the Lake District and had already been active in protecting footpaths and promoting public access to open countryside. After the flooding of Thirlmere in 1879 to create a large reservoir, he and his two colleagues became increasingly convinced that the only effective protection was outright ownership of land.

The purpose of the National Trust is to preserve areas of natural beauty and sites of historic interest by acquisition, holding them in trust for the nation and making them available for public access and enjoyment. Some of its properties have been acquired through purchase, but many have been donated. Nowadays it is not only one of the biggest landowners in the country, but also one of the most active conservation charities, protecting well over half a million acres of land, including over 500 miles of coastline and a large number of historic properties (houses, castles and gardens) in England, Wales and Northern Ireland. (There is a separate National Trust for Scotland, which was set up in 1931.)

Furthermore, once a piece of land has come under Trust ownership, it is difficult for its status to be altered. As a result of Parliamentary legislation in 1907, the Trust was given the right to declare its property inalienable, so ensuring that in any dispute it can appeal directly to Parliament.

As it works towards its dual aims of conserving areas of attractive countryside and encouraging greater public access (not easy to reconcile in this age of mass tourism), the Trust provides an excellent service to walkers by creating new concessionary paths and waymarked trails, by maintaining stiles and footbridges and by combating the over increasing problem of footpath erosion.

For details of membership, contact the National Trust at the address on page 78.

The Ramblers' Association

No organisation works more actively to protect and extend the rights and interests of walkers in the countryside than the Ramblers' Association. Its aims (summarised here) are clear: to foster a greater knowledge, love and care of the countryside; to assist in the protection and enhancement of public rights of way and areas of natural beauty; to work for greater public access to the countryside and to encourage more people to take up rambling as a healthy, recreational activity.

It was founded in 1935 when, following the setting up of a National Council of Ramblers' Federation in 1931, a number of federations earlier formed in London, Manchester, the Midlands and elsewhere came together to create a more effective pressure group, to deal with such contemporary problems as the disappearance and obstruction of footpaths, the prevention of access to open mountain and moorland and increasing hostility from landowners. This was the era of the mass trespasses, when there were sometimes violent confrontations between ramblers and gamekeepers, especially on the moorlands of the Peak District.

Since then the Ramblers' Association has played an influential role in preserving and

Wolsingham, County Durham

developing the national footpath network, supporting the creation of National Parks and encouraging the designation and way-marking of long-distance footpaths.

Our freedom to walk in the countryside is precarious, and requires constant vigilance. As well as the perennial problems of footpaths being illegally obstructed, disappearing through lack of use or extinguished by housing or road construction, new dangers can spring up at any time.

It is to meet such problems and dangers that the Ramblers' Association exists and represents the interests of all walkers. The address to write to for information on the Ramblers' Association and how to become a member is given on page 78.

Walkers and the law

The average walker in a National Park or other popular walking area, armed with the appropriate Ordnance Survey map, reinforced perhaps by a guidebook giving detailed walking instructions, is unlikely to run into legal difficulties, but it is useful to know something about the law relating to public rights of way. The right to walk over certain parts of the countryside has developed over a long period of time, and how such rights came into being and how far they are protected by the law is a complex subject, fascinating in its own right, but too lengthy to be discussed here. The following comments are intended simply to be a helpful guide, backed up by the Countryside Access Charter, a concise summary of walkers' rights and obligations drawn up by the Countryside Commission.

Basically there are two main kinds of public rights of way: footpaths (for walkers only) and bridleways (for walkers, riders on

Cauldron Snout

horseback and pedal cyclists). Footpaths and bridleways are shown by broken green lines on Ordnance Survey Pathfinder and Outdoor Leisure maps and broken red lines on Landranger maps. There is also a third category, called byways or 'roads used as a public path': chiefly broad, walled tracks (green lanes) or farm roads, which walkers, riders and cyclists have to share, usually only occasionally, with motor vehicles. Many of these public paths have been in existence for hundreds of years and some even originated as prehistoric trackways and have been in constant use for well over 2,000 years.

The term 'right of way' means exactly what it says. It gives right of passage over what, in the vast majority of cases, is private land, and you are required to keep to the line of the path and not stray onto the land either side. If you inadvertently wander off the right of way — either because of faulty map-reading or because the route is not clearly indicated on the ground — you are technically trespassing and the wisest course is to ask the nearest available person (farmer or fellow walker) to direct you back to the correct route. There are stories of unpleasant confrontations between walkers and farmers at times, but in general most farmers are helpful and co-operative when responding to a genuine and polite request for assistance in route finding.

Obstructions can sometimes be a problem and probably the commonest of these is where a path across a field has been ploughed up. It is legal for a farmer to plough up a path provided that he restores it within two weeks, barring exceptionally bad weather. This does not always happen and here the walker is presented with a dilemma. Does he follow the line of the path, even if this inevitably means treading on crops, or does he use his common sense and walk around the edge of the field? The latter course of action often seems the best but, as this means that you would be trespassing, you are, in law, supposed to keep to the exact line of the path, avoiding unnecessary damage to crops. In the case of other obstructions which may block a path (illegal fences and locked gates etc.), common sense again has to be used in order to negotiate them by the easiest method (detour or removal). If you have any problems negotiating rights of way, you should report the matter to the Rights of Way Department of the relevant county, borough or metropolitan district council. They will then take action with the landowner concerned.

Apart from rights of way enshrined by law, there are a number of other paths available to walkers. Permissive or concessionary paths have been created where a landowner has given permission for the public to use a particular route across his land. The main problem with these is that, as they have been granted as a concession, there is no legal right to use them and therefore they can be extinguished at any time. In practice, many of these concessionary routes have been established on land owned either by large public bodies such as the Forestry Commission, or by a private one, such as the National Trust, and as these mainly encourage walkers to use their paths, they are unlikely to be closed unless a change of ownership occurs.

Walkers also have free access to Country Parks (except where requested to keep away from certain areas for ecological reasons, e.g. wildlife protection, woodland regeneration, safeguarding of rare plants etc.), canal towpaths and most beaches. By custom, though not by right, you are generally free to walk across the open and uncultivated higher land of mountain, moorland and fell, but this varies from area to area and from one season to another — grouse moors, for example, will be out of bounds during the breeding and shooting seasons and some open areas are used as Ministry of Defence firing ranges, for which reason access will be restricted. In some areas the situation has been clarified as a result of 'access agreements' between the landowners and either the county council or the National Park authority, which clearly define when and where you can walk over such open country.

Countryside Access Charter

Your rights of way are;
- Public footpaths — on foot only. Sometimes waymarked in yellow
- Bridleways — on foot, horseback and pedal cycle. Sometimes waymarked in blue
- Byways (usually old roads), most 'roads used as public paths' and, of course, public roads — all traffic has the right of way

Use maps, signs and waymarks to check rights of way. Ordnance Survey Pathfinder and Landranger maps show most public rights of way

On rights of way you can:
- take a pram, pushchair or wheelchair if practicable
- take a dog (on a lead or under close control)
- take a short route round an illegal obstruction or remove it sufficiently to get past

The Pennine Way near Eccles Cairn

You have a right to go for recreation to:
- public parks and open spaces — on foot
- most commons near older towns and cities — on foot and sometimes on horseback
- private land where the owner has a formal agreement with the local authority

In addition you can use the following by local or established custom or consent, but ask for advice if you are unsure:
- many areas of open country, such as moorland, fell and coastal areas, especially those in the care of the National Trust, and some commons
- some woods and forests, especially those owned by the Forestry Commission
- Country Parks and picnic sites
- most beaches
- canal towpaths
- some private paths and tracks

Consent sometimes extends to horse-riding and cycling

For your information:
- county councils and London boroughs maintain and record rights of way, and register commons
- obstructions, dangerous animals, harassment and misleading signs on rights of way are illegal and you should report them to the county council
- paths across fields can be ploughed, but must normally be reinstated within two weeks
- landowners can require you to leave land to which you have no right of access
- motor vehicles are normally permitted only on roads, byways and some 'roads used as public paths'

Key Map 1

Key Map 2

CONVENTIONAL SIGNS
1:25 000 or 2½ INCHES to 1 MILE

ROADS AND PATHS

Not necessarily rights of way

M I or A 6 (M)	M I or A 6 (M)	Motorway
A 31 (T)	A 31 (T)	Trunk road
A 35	A 35	Main road
B 3074	B 3074	Secondary road
A 35	A 35	Dual carriageway

Narrow roads with passing places are annotated

Road generally more than 4m wide

Road generally less than 4m wide

Other road, drive or track

Unfenced roads and tracks are shown by pecked lines

Path

RAILWAYS

Multiple track — Single track } Standard gauge

Narrow gauge

Siding

Cutting

Embankment

Tunnel

Road over & under

Level crossing; station

PUBLIC RIGHTS OF WAY

Public rights of way may not be evident on the ground

Public paths { Footpath / Bridleway

+ + + + + Byway open to all traffic

Road used as a public path

DANGER AREA
Firing and test ranges in the area
Danger!
Observe warning notices

The indication of a towpath in this book does not necessarily imply a public right of way
The representation of any other road, track or path is no evidence of the existence of a right of way

BOUNDARIES

— · — · — · — County (England and Wales)

— — — — District

–×– –×– –×– –×– London Borough

· · · · · · · · · · · Civil Parish (England)* Community (Wales)

— — — — — — Constituency (County, Borough, Burgh or European Assembly)

Coincident boundaries are shown by the first appropriate symbol

*For Ordnance Survey purposes County Boundary is deemed to be the limit of the parish structure whether or not a parish area adjoins

SYMBOLS

	Place { with tower	VILLA	Roman antiquity (AD 43 to AD 420)
	of { with spire, minaret or dome	Castle	Other antiquities
+	worship { without such additions		Site of antiquity
	Glasshouse; youth hostel	✗ 1066	Site of battle (with date)
	Bus or coach station		Gravel pit
	Lighthouse; lightship; beacon		Sand pit
	Triangulation station		Chalk pit, clay pit or quarry
	Triangulation point on { church or chapel / lighthouse, beacon / building; chimney		Refuse or slag heap
pylon pole	Electricity transmission line		Sloping wall

Water   Mud

Sand; sand & shingle

National Park or Forest Park Boundary

NT   National Trust open access

NT   National Trust limited access

NTS NTS   National Trust for Scotland

VEGETATION
Limits of vegetation are defined by positioning of the symbols but may be delineated also by pecks or dots

Coniferous trees

Non-coniferous trees

Coppice

Orchard

Scrub

Marsh, reeds, saltings

Bracken, rough grassland

In some areas bracken ( ) and rough grassland ( ) are shown separately

Heath

} Shown collectively as rough grassland on some sheets

In some areas reeds ( ) and saltings ( ) are shown separately

HEIGHTS AND ROCK FEATURES

50 / 285 } Determined by { ground survey / air survey

Surface heights are to the nearest metre above mean sea level. Heights shown close to a triangulation pillar refer to the ground level height at the pillar and not necessarily the summit.

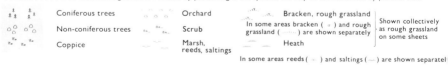

Vertical face

Loose rock   Boulders   Outcrop   Scree

Contours are at 5 metres vertical interval

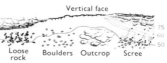

TOURIST INFORMATION

✟ Abbey, Cathedral, Priory	❁ Garden	☆ Other tourist feature
🐟 Aquarium	► Golf course or links	✕ Picnic site
Ⴟ Camp site	⊞ Historic house	🚃 Preserved railway
Caravan site	ℹ Information centre	🐎 Racecourse
Castle	🏎 Motor racing	Skiing
Cave	▣ Museum	Viewpoint
Country park	! Nature or forest trail	Wildlife park
Craft centre	Nature reserve	Zoo
P Parking		
PC Public Convenience (in rural areas)		

Castle
SAILING   Selected places of interest

Ancient Monuments and Historic Buildings in the care of the Secretary of State for the Environment which are open to the public

◆ ◆ National trail or Recreational Path
Long Distance Route (Scotland only)

T Public telephone

⊕ Mountain rescue post

Pennine Way   Named path

NATIONAL PARK Boundary of National Park access land
ACCESS LAND   Private land for which the National Park Planning Board have negotiated public access

◄ Access Point

WALKS

⚐1 Start point of walk   Featured walk   ➡ Route of walk   ▪▪▪▶ Alternative route

ABBREVIATIONS   1:25 000 or 2½ INCHES to 1 MILE also 1:10 000/1:10 560 or 6 INCHES to 1 MILE

BP,BS	Boundary Post or Stone	P	Post Office	A,R	Telephone, AA or RAC
CH	Club House	Pol Sta	Police Station	TH	Town Hall
F V	Ferry Foot or Vehicle	PC	Public Convenience	Twr	Tower
FB	Foot Bridge	PH	Public House	W	Well
HO	House	Sch	School	Wd Pp	Wind Pump
MP,MS	Mile Post or Stone	Spr	Spring		
Mon .	Monument	T	Telephone, public		

Abbreviations applicable only to 1:10 000/1:10 560 or 6 INCHES to 1 MILE

Ch	Church	GP	Guide Post	TCB	Telephone Call Box
F Sta	Fire Station	P	Pole or Post	TCP	Telephone Call Post
Fn	Fountain	S	Stone	Y	Youth Hostel

FOLLOW THE COUNTRY CODE
Enjoy the countryside and respect its life and work

Guard against all risk of fire	Take your litter home
Fasten all gates	Help to keep all water clean
Keep your dogs under close control	Protect wildlife, plants and trees
Keep to public paths across farmland	Take special care on country roads
Leave livestock, crops and machinery alone	Make no unnecessary noise
Use gates and stiles to cross fences, hedges and walls	

Reproduced by permission of the Countryside Commission

1 Kielder Water – the Bull Crag peninsula

Kielder Water from the Otterstone viewpoint

Start:	Bull Crag (the promontory due west of Tower Knowe Information Centre, Kielder Water)
Distance:	3 miles (4.75 km)
Approximate time:	1½ hours
Parking:	Bull Crag
Refreshments:	None
Ordnance Survey maps:	Landranger 80 (Cheviot Hills & Kielder Forest) and Explorer 1 (Kielder Water)

General description *A short and undemanding walk which allows the visitor to appreciate the beauty of Kielder Water as well as its vast scale. This is the largest man-made lake in Europe: covering 2,684 acres (1,086 ha) it is nine miles (14.5 km) long and contains 41,350 million gallons of water (188,000 million litres). The scheme was begun in 1976 and completed six years later. In summer a waterbus service allows visitors to explore remote shores out of the reach of roads. The route does not dwell overlong amongst pine trees and is well waymarked in the usual Forestry Commission manner. It will be a favourite both with children and dogs.*

There are orange waymarks to lead you round this route from the car park and picnic site at Bull Crag (there are toilets here too).

SCALE 1:25 000 or 2½ INCHES to 1 MILE

Start by returning up the track which has brought you to the car park and turn right at the top following a sign to Otterstone viewpoint. The road forks on two occasions; bear left each time to reach the car park at Otterstone. The viewpoint (**A**), which certainly provides a splendid vista of lake and forest, is set amongst a lovely group of ancient Scots pines. From here it is easy to appreciate that this is the largest forest in Britain, covering about 200 square miles (518 square km). There were few trees in this vast area of moorland when planting began in 1926.

The path doglegs down to the shore, crossing a fence to head eastwards (for a short stretch through trees where there are evil-looking redcap toadstools). After this the path joins a section of the old main road which once ran through the valley of the North Tyne. Most of it was covered by water many years ago, and in fact this portion too vanishes below the waters of the reservoir. However our way is to the right, continuing along the shore towards the Headland. There is a good view of the dam from here as the path threads through heather. The dam is ¾ mile (1 km) long and 169 feet (52 m) high.

Having skirted the Headland the path leaves the waterside (**B**) to head into the forest. If you are very fortunate you may catch a glimpse of a great spotted woodpecker or even a crossbill amongst the trees here. The latter's crossed mandibles allow it to extract pine seeds from tightly closed cones. Coal tits and redpolls also flourish in pine forests. A large cleared area on the left allows a glimpse of the reservoir. At the end of the felled section the way bears left to dive into a short, very gloomy, stretch through the trees. This emerges into a firebreak which is rather boggy. The busy Whickhope marina can be seen below. The path twists through the mature pines which overlook this creek, soon reaching the Bull Crag picnic site again.

2 Blanchland

Start: Blanchland

Distance: 3 ½ miles (5.5 km)

Approximate time: 2 hours

Parking: Blanchland

Refreshments: Pub and café at Blanchland

Ordnance Survey maps: Landranger 87 (Hexham & Haltwhistle), Pathfinders 560, NY 85/95 (Allendale Town & Blanchland) and 570, NY 84/94 (Allenheads & Rookhopo)

General description Blanchland is justly famous as one of England's most beautiful villages. Situated in the wooded valley of the River Derwent (which here forms the boundary between Northumberland and County Durham), its honey-coloured houses (made from the fabric of the monastery) huddle around the ancient abbey church. The moors rise up on all sides. Its famous hotel, the Lord Crewe Arms, was once the guesthouse of the abbey and provides refreshments for walkers in the bar. Look out for its ghosts! The short walk takes you up to the open moorland and then drops to the Derwent for a riverbank walk back to Blanchland.

Turn left out of the car park and climb up the lane through woodland. From April until July the verges and hedgerows are ablaze with a glorious variety of wild flowers. The lane is made-up as far as Shildon, where on the left you can see the remains of old lead mine workings. Above Shildon the lane becomes a farm track but the walking is still comfortable. Look for northern marsh orchids in the ditch on the right as the track emerges into more open country.

Pennypie House appears ahead. This farm apparently got its name from the pies it baked (and sold for a penny) to the miners who used the track to get to their work. Pass through a gate onto the open moor (**A**) but resist the temptation to continue to climb further on this track, and instead turn to the left at the gate onto another track which runs southwards with the wall on the left. The views from here over the village to the moorland on the other side of Derwent valley are magical and the going easy on a grassy path. Lapwings and curlews nest in the tussocky moorland here; the latter, with its curved beak and spine-tingling, unearthly call, is the symbol of the Northumberland National Park.

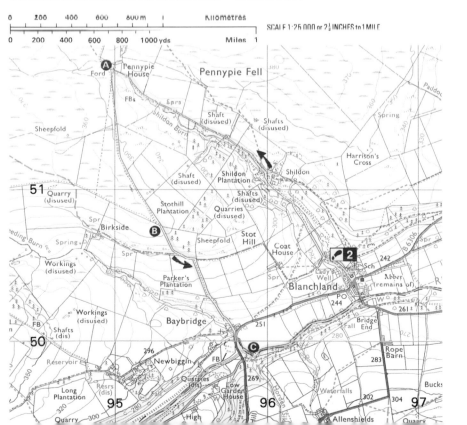

Blanchland

3 Allen Banks

Start:	Allen Banks, near Bardon Mill
Distance:	3 miles (4.75 km)
Approximate time:	1½ hours
Parking:	National Trust car park and picnic site at Allen Banks
Refreshments:	None
Ordnance Survey maps:	Landrangers 86 (Haltwhistle, Bewcastle & Alston) and 87 Hexham & Haltwhistle), Pathfinders 546, NY 66/76 (Haltwhistle & Gilsland) and 547, NY 86/96 (Hexham & Haydon Bridge)

A gasline pumping station on the right heralds the end of this too-brief moorland interlude. Follow the metalled lane downhill from this point (**B**): it descends very steeply to the road at Baybridge but there are still impresssive panoramas to enjoy *en route*.

At the road turn right and walk past the Carricks picnic site to the bridge. Turn left (**C**) just before the bridge onto the footpath which follows the north bank of the Derwent. A causeway of duckboarding takes the path to the riverbank, and it then runs close by the river through woodland and meadows to Blanchland. It is easy to linger on this part of the walk, especially on a warm day. There is nothing more soothing than the sound of rushing water and sunlight highlighting its passage through a canopy of overhanging trees.

At the bridge at Blanchland turn left to walk through the village to the car park, passing the Lord Crewe Arms, the medieval gatehouse, and the abbey church on the way. Most of the fabric of the abbey was incorporated into the village buildings when Blanchland was rebuilt as a model village in the mid-eighteenth century. Only the chancel of the abbey church was saved and this was adopted as the parish church. It was restored again in Victorian times. Interesting coffin lids are to be seen in the floor of the transept: two depict abbots who hold their pastoral staff while the third shows the huntsman to the abbey, Robert de Egylston, with the tools of his trade, a horn, arrow and sword.

A red-haired monk is one of two ghosts which haunt the Lord Crewe Arms. The other is the shade of Dorothy Forster who helped her brother Tom, a Jacobite general, to evade pursuers by concealing him in a priest's hole. Earlier she had helped him escape from Newgate Prison. Her ghost appears to implore visitors to take a message to him in France, where he eventually took refuge.

General description The National Trust have done a wonderful job in opening up the footpaths in and around the 200 acres (81 ha) of Allen Banks. In its own way this property is almost as spectacular as Cragside, the River Allen having cut a precipitous gorge here on its course to join with the Tyne. Fine trees grow by the river and on the steep sides of its valley, making excellent habitats for many birds, including woodpeckers. Allen Banks is also one of the last refuges of the red squirrel in this country, though you will be fortunate indeed if you see one. An extra 1½-mile excursion can be made to the tarn in Morralee Wood; it is Northumberland's answer to Tarn Hows — a really idyllic spot.

The National Trust's car park was once the walled garden of Ridley Hall, seat of one of the most celebrated of Northumbrian families. Take the riverside path and after ½ mile (0.75 km) — before the bridge — look for steps on the right which lead to a steep path climbing to the top of the steep-sided valley. A stile here gives access into Ridley Park (you can just see the house). Do not cross this but turn left (**A**) onto the path which runs along the side of the park fence.

The path still climbs, though not so severely, as it passes fine specimens of beech and oak. The River Allen is now far below. Sheep graze on the other side of the fence and there is a super-abundance of pheasants.

For a while there are trees to both sides of the path but eventually the fence returns on the right. When the way ahead is stopped by a steep ravine look for the Bone-floor Viewpoint, a circular clearing of about 10 feet (3 m) diameter floored with the knuckle-bones of sheep. It is well camouflaged by a growth of moss. Take the steep, zigzag path down here by the side of the stream and be especially careful if the steps are wet or covered with leaves. Turn right onto the riverside path, crossing the footbridge (**B**).

The path winds beneath magnificent, tall pines. A diversion can be made to the right through Briarwood Bank Nature Reserve (Northumberland Wildlife Trust). Dogs are not allowed, however.

Cross the footbridge over the small stream and continue along the riverside path to the suspension bridge (**C**) which provides an exciting way over the Allen. On the eastern bank take the lane from Plankey Mill which climbs up steeply, and then the track which forks off to the left. After 50 yards (46 m) a stile leads onto the riverside footpath which passes through a meadow and then runs alongside a beautifully rebuilt stone wall. After a pastoral interlude the path comes again to the gorge. Keep to the lower path which zigzags around enormous boulders which have fallen from above. Steps lead to a high path above the crags which looks adventurous.

Our way close to the rushing waters of the lovely river should not be hurried. Herons will flap lazily from their favourite fishing haunts. Dippers hop from rock to rock, and occasionally you may see or hear a large salmon leap at a fly (this stretch of river is a sanctuary for fish). In places the path is being undermined: take great care when it becomes very narrow approaching the bridge. This route does not require the bridge (**D**) to be crossed (if the planks are wet this can demand steady nerves).

If you wish to make a 1½-mile (2.5 km) detour to visit Morralee Wood and the enchanting tarn within it, take the route marked with white-painted tops (the route back from the tarn is not marked). Take the steps to the right and then turn right again following the posts and (on two occasions) a rock engraved 'To Tarn'. Keep climbing up steps to cross the upper path mentioned earlier and keep straight on as the view opens up over the Tyne valley. After more pleasant walking the path does a U-turn and climbs steeply through tall pines to reach the lovely tarn. Keep on the path to the right of the tarn, and spare a moment to enjoy the view: Ridley Hall can be seen through the trees. The way back owes much to instinct. There is a maze of paths here but no white posts as guides. The main path climbs steeply from the tarn. Take this and keep straight on through avenues of rhododendrons to reach a path running along the side of the valley. At first this seems as though it may lead you back to Plankey Mill, but eventually it plunges down to a lower path which follows the river back to the bridge at (**D**).

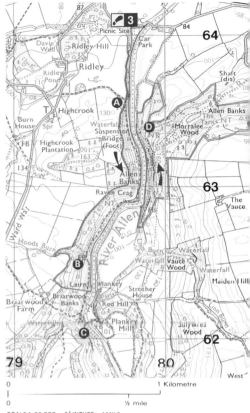

SCALE 1:25 000 or 2½ INCHES to 1 MILE

From (**D**) the path along the eastern bank of the River Allen runs through field and meadow to reach the road bridge. Pass beneath this to find the gate onto the road and then cross the bridge to reach the car park

The top path at Allen Banks

4 Cox Green and Penshaw Hill

Start:	Cox Green, 3 miles (4.75 km) west of Sunderland
Distance:	3 ½ miles (5.5 km)
Approximate time:	1 ½ hours
Parking:	Cox Green
Refreshments:	Pubs at Cox Green and close to point (**C**) at Penshaw
Ordnance Survey maps:	Landranger 88 (Tyneside & Durham) and Pathfinder 562, NZ 25/35 (Washington & Chester-le-Street)

General description *Many people must wonder about the monument on top of Penshaw Hill as they dash past it on the A19. It is a magnificent viewpoint (you can even see the distinctive shapes of the Cheviots from here on a good day) and it is also celebrated as being the place where the Lambton Worm lurked. The grooves on the hill (which are difficult to discern) are supposed to have been made when it coiled*

The Penshaw monument

itself around it. Other parts of the walk use the River Wear Trail, a fine network of paths.

Cox Green is a delightful Wearside beauty spot with a large car park opposite the Oddfellows Arms pub. Until the latter part of the nineteenth century it was a busy port handling timber, coal and sandstone. Ships were built and repaired (there is still a boatyard for pleasure craft), the last being launched into the waters of the Wear in 1862. Turn left at the river and follow the road past the handful of houses. Beyond these there is a narrow riverside path leading towards the Victoria Viaduct which was opened in 1838 and takes the east coast main line across the valley. On the left there used to be tunnels

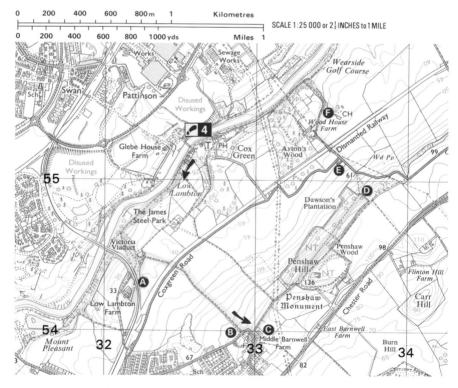

which brought sandstone down to the riverside loading staithes from the quarries at Low Lambton. Turn left off the riverside path at the noticeboard before the viaduct: this is James Steel Park named after the former Lord Lieutenant of Durham, Sir James Steel, who was also the first chairman of the Washington Development Corporation. It extends for 2½ miles (4 km) on both sides of the river.

Pass under the railway by the tunnel and then bear left to pass round the south and east sides of Low Lambton Farm (it feels like their front garden). Go under the railway again by the arch on the right (**A**) and on the other side turn left along the field edge. On meeting the hedgerow of the next field turn right towards the monument and follow a much clearer path to the left of the hedge towards another railway embankment. Climb this to cross the old trackbed and then go down the other side to cross the road too. The well used path runs up the right side of the field below electricity lines. At the top (**B**) turn left onto the road and then left again (**C**) onto a path before new bungalows (if you need refreshment follow the road for a few more steps to reach a couple of pubs).

There are magnificent views from the path and even better ones from the monument itself. The Nissan factory is a prominent landmark. Unexpectedly, the monument is roofless, uncompleted. It was built in the form of a Doric temple, perhaps a copy of the Temple of Theseus in Athens, to the memory of Radical Jack Lambton, the Liberal politician who died in 1840.

The story of the Lambton Worm is one of the most famous of north country legends. John, the heir to the Lambton estates in medieval times, is said to have slain the monstrous worm, but invoked a curse under which nine lords of Lambton died unexpected deaths. The terraces on the hill said to have been caused by the worm coiling itself around it are best seen on the hill's south side. (Worm Hill close to the Victoria Viaduct at Fatfield on the north side of the Wear is also claimed to be a resting-place of the serpent.)

From the monument return to the path below which runs through the woods on the lower slopes of the hill. After the stile which leads the path out of the woods (**D**) cross the meadow diagonally to its lower left corner. Carry straight on along the road, passing a 'Private Road' sign when the Cox Green road goes off to the left opposite an old school (**E**).

Follow this lane round towards the golf club but leave it to take a path on the left when the drive bears to the right (**F**). This descends to the river through a peaceful, wooded little valley. Turn left at the riverbank to complete the walk.

5 Doddington Moor

Start:	Doddington
Distance:	4 miles (6.5 km)
Approximate time:	2 hours
Parking:	Lay-by at Doddington village cross or off-road in lane opposite
Refreshments:	None
Ordnance Survey maps:	Landranger 75 (Berwick-upon-Tweed), Pathfinders 463, NT 83/93 (Coldstream) and 464, NU 03 (Lowick)

General description *It's not difficult to see why Doddington Moor was popular with prehistoric Northumbrians. Although breezy, its wide horizons gave plenty of warning of enemies approaching. It makes a good walk – a gentle ascent on a firm track is followed by stretches across pasture and heather. Although the moor is littered with prehistoric monuments, only the larger ones are obvious on the ground.*

Refer to map overleaf.

Take the lane up from the stone cross towards Wooler Golf Club. As for so much of this walk, there are fine views of the Cheviots, though on the way up the hill you have to pause and turn to appreciate them.

The lane goes off to the right to the golf club: our way lies ahead through the gate onto a sandy track which continues to climb. However, it dips briefly by sheep pens where a shepherd's mobile home stands close by. New plantations have been established on the left which in later years will screen the views in this direction. As the track levels out look for a gate on the right (**A**) with a sign to Weetwood Hill and take this path across a large pasture. Head to the left of the clump of trees on the skyline, and when you meet the wall at the top turn right to reach this spinney (called Kitty's Plantation). At this point (**B**) you may look back to see the most obvious of Doddington's Bronze Age monuments – the fort known as the Ringses. Less obvious are the host of rocks carved with cup and ring symbols to be found on the fellsides around the village. There are said to be more of these within a five-mile radius of the village than anywhere else in Britain.

Keep the wall to the left after a gate takes the path onto open moorland. There should be a stone circle at the footpath crossways (**C**) though it is not very apparent on the

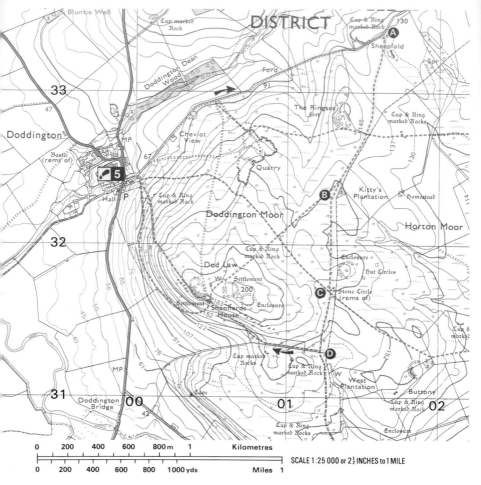

Bluntie Well
Cup marked Rock
Cup & Ring marked Rock
130
A
Sheepfold
Spr
Doddington Dean
Doddington Wood
Ford
91
33
47
The Ringses Fort
Cup & Ring marked Rocks
145
137
130
Doddington
MP
Cheviot View
Bastle (rems of)
5
67
Quarry
Hall P
Cup & Ring marked Rock
Kitty's Plantation
Homestead
Horton Moor
114
B
Doddington Moor
32
Cup & Ring marked Rock
Dod Law
Enclosure
Hut Circles
W Settlement
200
Settlement
1834 Shepherds House
Enclosure
Stone Circle (rems of)
C
122
107
91
76
Cup marked Rocks
61
D
Cup & Ring marked Rock W
West Plantation
Buttony
MP
31
Doddington Bridge 00
Cave
01
Cup & Ring marked Rock 02
42
Cup & Ring marked Rocks
Enclosure

| 0 | 200 | 400 | 600 | 800 m | 1 | Kilometres |
| 0 | 200 | 400 | 600 | 800 | 1000 yds | Miles 1 |

SCALE 1:25 000 or 2½ INCHES to 1 MILE

ground. The path threads its way through high bracken (its route is easier to distinguish in winter when it has died back). Continue to keep close to the wall. Two lone pines in the field beyond the fence ahead stand as an excellent foreground to a Cheviot panorama.

Turn right at the fence (**D**) and follow it until the Shepherd's House comes into sight. Make for this on the path up the bracken-covered hillside of Dod Law. There are interesting traditions attached to the area just

The Shepherd's House on Dod Law

to the south of this hilltop. The Devil is said to have hanged his grandmother over a tall free-standing block of stone here which is grooved by the chains he used. Close to this is Cuddy's Cave, used by St Cuthbert when he was a young shepherd. A little further to the south, at the confluence of the rivers Till and Glen, King Arthur fought the first of his twelve great battles.

Walk past the front of the Shepherd's House (it is a landmark from many points in the Cheviots) and continue along the flank of the hill (do not turn right to follow the enclosure wall). There is a thoughtfully sited seat on the right below a golf tee if you care to rest to enjoy the view.

The ruined tower in the farmyard of Doddington Hall below is a bastle, which in the Borders is a diminutive of castle. It dates from 1584, a very late year for the building of such a stronghold. The path follows a fence and a line of thorn trees down to a stile onto the golf club lane. Turn left, back to the main road.

6 Simonside

Start:	Simonside Forest Park, near Rothbury
Distance:	4 miles (6.5 km)
Approximate time:	2½ hours
Parking:	Picnic site off the road to Great Tosson, 3 miles (4.75 km) south-west of Rothbury off the Hexham road (B6342)
Refreshments:	None
Ordnance Survey maps:	Landranger 81 (Alnwick & Morpeth) and Pathfinder 511, NZ 09/19 (Longhorsley & Simonside Hills)

General description The Simonside Hills have a distinctly different appearance to that of the Cheviots. While the latter are gently rounded these are often likened to a series of choppy breakers. They are darker and more rugged hills than their grander neighbours and from them the views are breathtaking. Altogether this is one of the Forestry Commission's most enjoyable walks. Although the first part of the route is upwards through the ranks of pines, interest is held by the viewpoints which occur with regularity. *Add to this the usual advantage of having the route impeccably waymarked and you have a perfect recipe for a splendid couple of hours or so.*

Before starting study the map at the picnic site. The one described here is the red route, the Simonside Ridge Walk. All the routes start along the same track, though the easier, green, route soon departs. After about twenty minutes steady climb on a forest track you come to a seat which overlooks a fine vista of Coquetdale to the Cheviots. The Cheviot is the highest summit to be seen at 2,674 feet (815 m) with Hedgehope to its right, second highest at 2,343 feet (714 m). A little further (**A**) and a short diversion is offered on the left to Little Church Rock. The scramble to the top is rewarding: the tor-like crag is an even better viewpoint than the seat.

Returning to the red route, this soon becomes more of a forest path — twisting up through the trees (mainly lodgepole pines) over rough boulders. It emerges on a drive on the open hillside, which in turn is left when a path makes for the 'dour ridge' of Simonside itself. Rock climbers enjoy tackling these crags in difficult ways but the official route is a gentle scramble which results in the capture of the summit (**B**) at 1,409 feet (430 m) where a cairn offers shelter for the enjoyment of the view — the Cheviots in one direction, the entire stretch of Northumberland's coastline in the other, from Tweed to Tyne. The

---

0   200   400   600   800 m   1   Kilometres

0   200   400   600   800   1000 yds   Miles   1

SCALE 1:25 000 or 2½ INCHES to 1 MILE

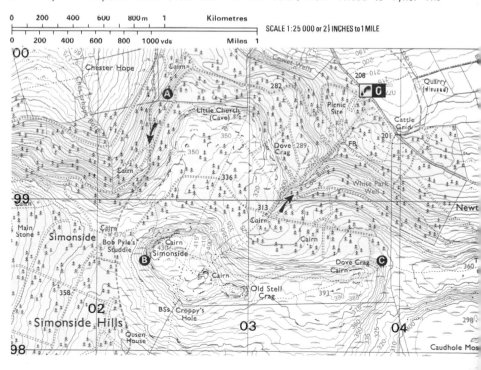

Coquet, the queen of rivers, can be seen in the near-distance, flowing through the town of Rothbury. Simonside is the haunt of mischievous elves known as 'duegars' – perhaps they were responsible for carving the mysterious cup and ring symbols onto rocks in this locality, just to perplex humans!

The path follows the ridge of fell sandstone, its particles of quartz glistening in the light. It is easy to understand how grouse came by their name as they whirr away with raucous complaints. Heather burning takes place on Simonside as it does throughout the moorland of northern England in order to provide tender shoots to feed both grouse and sheep. It is carried out on a rotational basis.

On the right is Old Stell Crag whose summit is not climbed. It was the site of the Simonside Beacon which in the days of the reivers was lit to give warning of raids by the Scots. The waymarks lead on to Dove Crag (**C**) which gives a view of Rothbury and Cragside. The waymarked path descends from the moor after Dove Crag, following alternating sections of broad drives and then narrow paths which wind down steeply through the trees, returning quite suddenly to the picnic site.

The view from Dove Crag

7 Craster and Dunstanburgh Castle

Start:	Craster
Distance:	4½ miles (7.25 km)
Approximate time:	2½ hours
Parking:	National Trust car park at Craster
Refreshments:	Pubs and seasonal café at Craster
Ordnance Survey maps:	Landrangers 75 (Berwick-upon-Tweed) and 81 (Alnwick & Morpeth), Pathfinder 477, NU 21/22 (Embleton & Alnmouth)

General description *The trouble with really excellent short walks is that they become overcrowded: thus choose your time carefully. There are seldom crowds about early in the morning when the sea-light on the castle can be magical (as can that of late evening). The drawback to these times is that the opening time for the castle is 10 a.m. and it is closed in the evening.*

The National Trust car park at Craster occupies the old quarry. This quarry, like most of the village, was owned by the family which gave the place its name. They lived in Craster for more than seven centuries. The whinstone produced by the quarry was sent to London and other great cities where it was used as kerbstones.

A path leads from the quarry to the harbour. Turn northwards from here having taken in the charm of the small fishing village, famous for its delicious oak-smoked kippers. A handful of picturesque cobles, the distinctive craft of Northumbrian fishermen, usually rest in the harbour – once it was full of them. Craster harbour was built in 1906 by the family as a monument to Captain Craster who was killed during the British military expedition to Tibet in 1904.

The walk to the castle is on springy turf (worn in places) with a platform of dolerite on the seaward side providing countless rock pools which children love to explore, discovering hermit crabs, anemones and periwinkles. This rock is volcanic in origin, intruded between other strata to form the distinctive 'sill' which at its seaward end makes a dramatic, and very secure, site for the castle (**A**). The path divides at the approach to the castle: take the right fork if

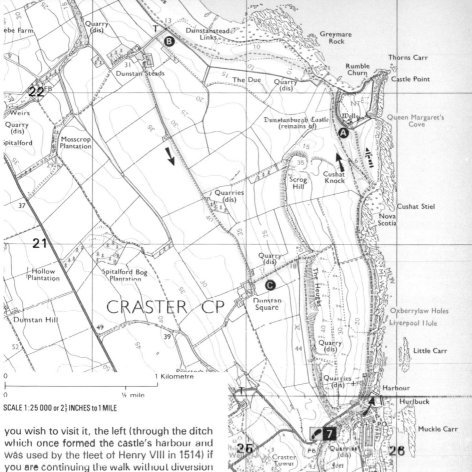

you wish to visit it, the left (through the ditch which once formed the castle's harbour and was used by the fleet of Henry VIII in 1514) if you are continuing the walk without diversion from the right of way.

Walking beneath the walls of the stronghold emphasises the difficulties faced by those besieging the place. Dunstanburgh dates from 1314 and is by far the largest castle in the county, covering eleven acres (4½ ha). The precipitous dolerite crag forms the perfect defence on the two seaward sides as, indeed, it does to the west. Only to the south does the site lie open, and here the enormous gatehouse with its flanking towers defied attackers. During the Wars of the Roses it was twice besieged by the Earl of Warwick and was surrendered to him on each occasion. Subsequently it was left open to the elements, and these turned it into the picturesque ruin that we see today.

It is hardly surprising that Dunstanburgh has a ghost, a wandering knight named Sir Guy, said to bewail his failure to free a captive maiden, whose ghost appears on the ramparts on wild nights as a White Lady.

The footpath leads northwards beneath the forbidding walls to reach the sea at the south end of Embleton Bay. The seabirds here are mostly kittiwakes which nest on the rocky ledges of Gull Crag.

There follows a pleasant switchback walk along the crest of the sand-dunes, a golf course on the left. Note the fantastic swirl of lava on the shore at the beginning of this section just beyond the gate to Dunstanburgh Stead Links.

The route turns inland (B) on the slatted track which leads to the lane to Dunstan Steads. At the farm turn left again following the bridleway sign to Dunstan Square. This turns out to be a concrete track through fields and meadows, with good views of the castle to the left and the long sill. Before the concept of landscape conservation took hold much material was quarried from the sill for roadstone.

On the right is an endless vista of farmland. Trace coroon the brickwork of an old lime-kiln which, before the advent of artificial fertilisers, was vital for cultivation. At Dunstan Square (C) turn left to the Heughs, the local name for the volcanic ridge. Then turn right to walk southwards in its shelter, welcome when the east wind is blowing. The path is broad at first but becomes narrow after a kissing-gate. It emerges in Craster directly opposite the car park.

Start:	Dye House, south of Hexham
Distance:	4 ½ miles (7.25 km)
Approximate time:	2 ½ hours
Parking:	In lay-by on the east side of river by Dye House Bridge
Refreshments:	Pub at Whitley Chapel
Ordnance Survey maps:	Landranger 87 (Hexham & Haltwhistle) and Pathfinder 560, NY 85/95 (Allendale Town & Blanchland)

The Cobble Burn

General description *A short walk through woodland and meadow and along lanes to enjoy the countryside and wildlife of Hexhamshire. There are no severe gradients and this route has all the ingredients of an excellent Sunday afternoon stroll.*

The lay-by is on the south side of the bridge. Do not cross the bridge but instead take the track opposite the lay-by which drops down through trees to cross the stream by a ford. This is an idyllic place and it is easy to envy those living in the houses here. Climb up the steep drive on the other side of the stream to reach the road at Juniper and bear right along it through the hamlet.

At the first crossroads (**A**) take the lane to the right (a cul-de-sac) which drops down past an imposing modern bungalow (The Peth) to reach Devil's Water. Turn right over the footbridge and then right again (**B**) on the path through the woods towards Whitley Chapel. This is an excellent stretch through lovely trees which must be at their most

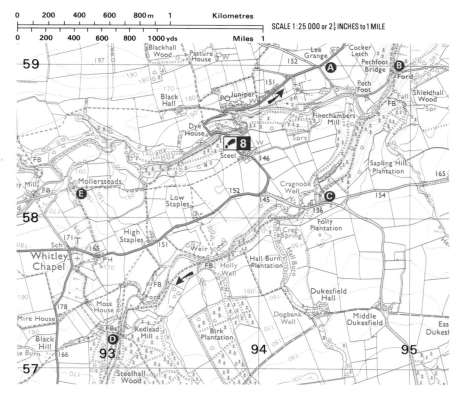

beautiful in spring or autumn. Heron's Burn is crossed and shortly after this the trees are conifers. The path has climbed now so that Devil's Water is far below. Unfortunately, it suffers a little from being churned up by hooves and the tyres of mountain bikes. At Cragnook the path emerges into a field. There are magnificent pine trees on the right. Go through the gate ahead into a recent planting of mixed trees. This track leads almost immediately to the road (**C**); here turn right.

After a few yards down the road take the track on the left opposite the house to enter more woodland. Again a stream is on the right, sometimes out of sight but usually audible. This is a lovely stretch particularly rich in birdlife. You might even see a kingfisher as after a footbridge the path runs through meadows by the stream.

At Redlead Mill pass the house and take the footbridge on the right (**D**) (do not go through the gate into Steelhall Wood). Beyond the footbridge there is another bridge over a mini-ravine. After this take the path ahead which climbs through resinous trees and then descends to the Cobble Burn which is crossed by a wooden footbridge. From here the way ascends to a stone stile which gives onto a meadow. Here you are faced by Moss House on the right and Mire House to the left. Keep the former close to the right and head straight across the meadow towards a black barn. There is a stile just to the left of this. Cross the boggy ground on the far side of the stile and take the farm track which leads to the road at Whitley Chapel. Turn right past the chapel, then right again to reach the Click-em-in pub.

The footpath continues through the yard and garden of the pub; a bench is usually strategically placed so that it is easy to cross the stile over the garden fence into the field and on to the path leading to Mollersteads. On the far side of the meadow by the pub there are steps taking the right of way over a fence. The top of these steps provides a good viewpoint for the surrounding countryside.

The path now drops down to Mollersteads (**E**), passing through a gateway to the right of the house to head eastwards with a line of oaks and then a fence to the right. At the second gateway cross the fence on the right and continue with it on the left. Follow it down to where it meets another fence (from the right) by fir trees. Go over the fence here, across a stone footbridge and turn left onto a path through trees. Felling has meant that the line of the right of way is indistinct here as the path drops down with the edge of the wood on the left. Where the path divides fork left to follow the course of the Rowley Burn through the woods back to the bridge at the starting point.

9 Alwinton and Clennell Street

Start: Alwinton

Distance: 4 ½ miles (7.25 km)

Approximate time: 2 hours

Parking: National Park car park at Alwinton

Refreshments: Pub at Alwinton

Ordnance Survey maps: Landranger 80 (Cheviot Hills & Kielder Forest) and Pathfinder 499, NT 80/90 (Harbottle)

General description *The River Alwin, a tributary of the Coquet, flows southwards through a steep-sided valley above Alwinton, the most important of the 'ten towns of Coquetdale' (historically, a loose defensive alliance of local communities). It stands at a meeting-point of several drovers' roads and border tracks, amongst them Clennell Street, which surmounted the Cheviot ridge to link England with Scotland. This walk follows the ancient thoroughfare up from the village, leaving it to drop to the river itself and returning to Alwinton by its banks.*

Refer to map overleaf.

From the car park turn left and pass the Rose and Crown pub to reach the village green. Sir Walter Scott stayed at the Rose and Crown when he was researching *Rob Roy*. Cross the footbridge over the Housedon Beck on the far side of the green which leads to the south end of Clennell Street. This is an ancient drovers' road which comes south from Scotland via Russell's Cairn on the border fence. There were many tracks like this through the highlands of northern England, and though most had their origins in medieval or even prehistoric times, their heyday was in the eighteenth and nineteenth centuries before the advent of railways. Then 100,000 cattle would be driven south from Scotland each year using these 'informal' tracks which avoided inconvenient and expensive turnpikes. They were also favoured by smugglers who would carry 'grey hens' to remote farms and cottages. This was their name for the flagons containing 'innocent whisky' (i.e. duty-free) which they sold to remote farms and cottages.

Clennell Street becomes a very rough track beyond the farm (on the left) climbing quite steeply, passing to the right of an Iron Age hill-fort (there is another on the opposite side of the valley) and by the cottage named Clennellstreet.

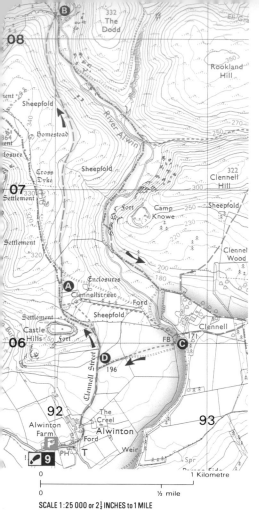

Near the top of the hill (**A**) the ancient drove road goes through a gate on the left: we leave it here to fork right to a stile over the fence. Another stile follows almost immediately. This is a bridleway (hence the blue waymarks) which follows the contours along the side of the valley. The landscape is enchanting, the Clennell estate and the snug village of Alwinton beyond the river enfolded by the soft curves of Cheviot hills with the dark mass of Simonside as a backdrop. Where the path divides follow the left fork: the way is marked by frequent posts.

The path soon begins to dip down to the valley and the red road which runs by the river. At the bottom (**B**) turn sharply to the right onto the road to return to Alwinton. Its grassy verges allow easy walking and there is usually the opportunity to spot a heron or two, with dippers and leaping fish. The scree slopes on the other side of the valley below Rookland Hill owe their origins to extremes of temperature over the many centuries which have passed since the Ice Age. Constant freezing and thawing has split the rock into millions of unstable fragments, always poised to avalanche down if disturbed from a slope that is almost sheer. Trees once held this treacherous surface together but these have long since vanished under the persistent grazing of sheep.

Opposite Clennell there is a blue footbridge on the right (**C**) which carries a footpath across the river. Take this path and after the bridge climb a steep bank to reach a stile. The path then climbs up, crossing two fields to reach Clennell Street again (**D**). Turn left to return to Alwinton.

The valley of the River Alwin

10 West Dipton Valley and High Yarridge

Start: Dipton Mill, near Hexham

Distance: 5½ miles (8.75 km). Shorter version 3 miles (4.75 km)

Approximate time: 3 hours (1½ hours for shorter version)

Parking: Parking space opposite Dipton Mill Inn

Refreshments: Pub at Dipton Mill

Ordnance Survey maps: Landranger 87 (Hexham & Haltwhistle) and Pathfinder 547, NY 86/96 (Hexham & Haydon Bridge)

General description This is a double figure-of-eight shaped route based on an excellent pub. Its course offers lots of alternatives; both shorter and longer versions

climb out of the valley so that walkers can enjoy fine vistas of the rolling countryside just to the south of the town. The shorter route follows the West Dipton Burn westwards, omitting the diversion around the racecourse to High Yarridge.

Cross the bridge from Dipton Mill Inn and take the path on the left leading into West Dipton Woods. This is a delightful winding path through the trees, often close to the chuckling waters of the burn, which flows over cataracts in places. The path may be muddy after rain.

Emerge from the wood to find a paddock on the right. The path skirts the left side of this. Paths diverge at the upper end of the paddock (**A**).

For the shorter version of the walk, continue to follow the stream to the footbridge at (D), cross the bridge and follow the main route after (D) overleaf.

Turn right to climb out of the valley up a steep slope. Climb over a stile into a field and continue to climb with a fence to the right. Go through a gate on the right at the top of

```
0    200   400   600   800m   1        Kilometres
0    200   400   600   800   1000yds   Miles  1
```
SCALE 1:25 000 or 2½ INCHES to 1 MILE

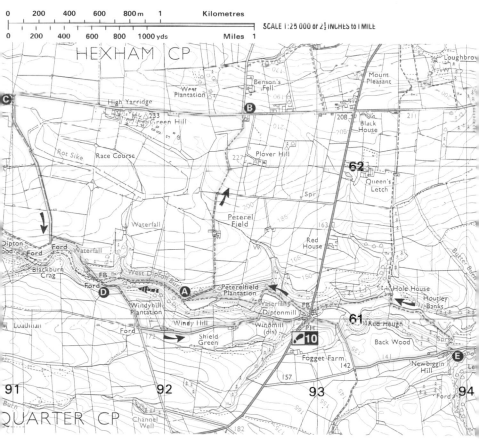

the field so that the fence is now on your left as you approach the farm, evocatively named Peterel Field. There is a lovely view back from here.

Pass to the left of the farm and onto a track towards Yarridge Road. Now there is a view of the racecourse on your left. Where the track bends sharply to the right towards fir trees keep straight on across the field ahead to a gate on the far side. Follow the edge of the next field and cross the following one, heading for the farmhouse on the right. Pass through the gate to the left of the farm to reach Yarridge Road (**B**).

Turn left here and walk along the high, quiet thoroughfare, passing the entrance to the racecourse on the left. To the right there are fine views of Hexham and the twin valleys of the Tyne. About ½ mile (0.75 km) beyond the racecourse entrance there is a drive (**C**) on the left to Blackhill. Take this bridleway forking left at the second gate to follow the waymark to West Dipton Burn. The lovely grassy path follows the western perimeter of the racecourse by old and twisted blackthorn trees. There are wide views in all directions.

Go through a gate into the woods and bear left on the path which follows the top of the valley, at first through beautiful mixed woodland (birch, beech and oak with a few Scots pines). You may be fortunate enough to see deer amongst these trees.

The path soon begins to zigzag down to the stream. Unfortunately, the timber has been stripped from the southern bank, but hopefully there will soon be replanting.

Cross the footbridge (**D**) and climb up the path which joins with a farm track at the top. This leads to the lane at Windy Hill where we turn left and follow it back to Dipton Mill past some lovely holly hedges which when they are berried provide a colourful foreground to the lovely view across the valley.

Pause for a pint if you like at the inn. Otherwise cross the road to the track opposite which leads up to the lane to Newbiggin Hill. Turn left onto this lane and immediately after the house on the right go through an unwaymarked gate on the left (**E**) and descend on a faint zigzag track to the path which leads westwards along the bank of the stream. This is another pleasant stretch of footpath which passes through a long meadow to a footbridge at its end. Cross this and climb to the top of the field to the wall below Hole House. Turn left to keep this wall (and then a fence) on your right. Cross the stile at the end of another long streamside meadow onto a track through a small wood with the West Dipton Burn close on the left. There is a fine view of a waterfall just before this path reaches the road close to the bridge. Cross the bridge to return to the starting point.

11 Hadrian's Wall from Steel Rigg

Start:	Steel Rigg (1 mile (1.5 km) north of National Park Information Centre at Once Brewed, Military Road, Bardon Mill)
Distance:	5 miles (8 km)
Approximate time:	2½ hours
Parking:	National Park car park at Steel Rigg
Refreshments:	None
Ordnance Survey maps:	Landrangers 86 (Haltwhistle, Bewcastle & Alston) and 87 (Hexham & Haltwhistle), Pathfinder 546, NY 66/76 (Haltwhistle & Gilsland)

General description *This walk provides the opportunity of seeing the most dramatic stretch of Hadrian's Wall. Choose your time to undertake the route carefully – it is wise to avoid Bank Holiday afternoons! Early mornings or evenings are ideal, the low light dramatising the landscape and highlighting beautiful Crag Lough. Also avoid very windy days. The return leg on the north side of Hadrian's Wall is pleasant walking, with wonderful views of the wall and the whinstone ridge on which it was built.*

Pass through the kissing-gate in the lower-right corner of the car park and follow the path to the wall at Peel Gap. Steps help the steep ascent up to Peel Crags: this is the start of a switchback series of climbs and descents, perhaps the most photographed section of Hadrian's Wall. The spectacular view is of great interest geologically and strategically: the scarp of the Great Whin Sill is seen rising precipitously above Crag Lough while the dip slope falls gently away to the south. Look back too at the climb you have just made. It started from a vulnerable point in the wall, a gap where the Romans protected the wall by digging a deep ditch on its northern side. This can still be clearly seen.

The path soon drops down again, this time to a gap known as Cat Stairs where there is a tumble of stones which have fallen from the wall through the ages. The abundance of wild flowers which occupies this rocky habitat is attributed to the mortar which was used in the construction of the wall, its lime modifying the composition of the soil. Another climb follows and then a further steep descent, this time to Castle Nick.

The gap here was protected by Milecastle 39 which has been recently excavated. Although there are minor deviations in size and design, all of the milecastles along the wall had basic features in common. Built to accommodate eight soldiers, they were gatehouses allowing access from one side of the wall to the other. Thus the most important feature was the gatetower itself where the gates opened outwards on the north side of the wall. There were also living quarters, a storehouse, an oven and, in the north-east corner, steps leading to the battlemented parapet of the wall itself which was generally at least 19½ feet (6 m) high, from base to top. All this was surrounded on the south side by an enclosing bailey wall, also with parapet walk and crenellations and a gate on its south side. As the name implies, milecastles were situated a mile (1.5 km) apart.

The path climbs again and then drops down steps to a circular stone wall which protects a somewhat unhealthy-looking sycamore. Pass to the north side of the wall here following the waymarks. You are soon on the crags high above the Lough. Heather-topped Barcombe Hill to the south is where the stone used in the wall was quarried. The communications tower to the north-west stands on the hill memorably named Hopealone.

The path descends through National Trust woodland (planted, not a natural feature) and skirts the boundary of Hotbank Farm to begin a taxing climb alongside the wall up to Hotbank Crags. The view from the top is a classic — one often used to illustrate Hadrian's Wall on postcards and brochures. To the west the wall snakes its way toward the horizon above the sparkling waters of Crag Lough (on a clear day the Lakeland summits of Blencathra and Skiddaw can be identified). To the north are the twin Greenlee and Broomlee Loughs, while

Housesteads car park can be seen ahead, heralding the most popular part of Hadrian's Wall with visitors.

For a short distance the wall is unreconstructed, and the path alongside dips down sharply to Ranishaw Gap which is where the Pennine Way joins with the wall to follow it westwards. There is a gate (A) and steps on the left. Cross the wall by these but do not follow the waymark which points out the course of the Pennine Way towards Broomlee Lough north-eastwards. Instead follow the line of a broken-down wall (keeping it to the left) so that you are walking directly away from Hadrian's Wall at this point. When you arrive at what looks like a very ornate cattle-shelter (B) but was in fact a lime-kiln, turn left to follow a mini-escarpment westwards.

On the left there is a planting of conifers not shown on the map, while Greenlee Lough is on the right. Hadrian's Wall looks a forbidding defence-work from here which must have deterred many a raiding party. The walking is easy on springy turf. Another path joins from the right as ours bends to the left, and it turns again to reach a stone wall and a farm gate (C). Turn to the right following a waymark pointing across a large pasture (a notice requests people to walk in single file to avoid damaging the hay crop). From here the cliffs rearing above Crag Lough are truly impressive.

Cross the next meadow following a well used but still grassy path towards the crags on top of Steel Rigg. The path bends to the right to cross slightly boggy ground to reach a gate (but use the adjacent ladder-stile). The right of way now heads towards a cattle byre. Keep close to the wall on the right. Almost imperceptibly the path becomes a track. Pass Peatrigg Plantation and continue along the track until it reaches the road below Steel Rigg car park where you turn left to return to your car.

SCALE 1:30 120 or about 2 INCHES to 1 MILE

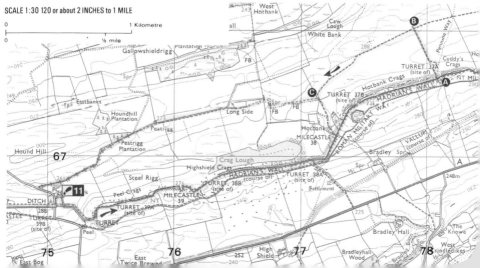

12 Above Rothbury

Start:	Rothbury
Distance:	5 miles (8 km)
Approximate time:	3 hours
Parking:	Riverside picnic site on the west side of Rothbury on B6341
Refreshments:	Pubs and cafés in Rothbury
Ordnance Survey maps:	Landranger 81 (Alnwick & Morpeth) and Pathfinder 500, NU 00/10 (Rothbury & Felton)

General description *Rothbury is a favourite centre for walkers wishing to explore the heart of Northumberland. The town is built on a series of natural south-facing terraces overlooking the River Coquet. Above the town some of the higher terraces were adapted by Lord Armstrong as carriage-drives after he built Cragside; this walk utilises parts of these. After the initial stiff climb, the walking is mainly easy and varied with fine views over the town and valley.*

Take the path up to the road from the middle of the picnic site. Turn right to the County Hotel and then sharp left up a road which makes a gentle ascent of the hill (Beggars Rigg), giving good views of the valley.

Continue past Hillside Road on the right to the houses where the road levels. Look for a bungalow called Roding on the right. Between Roding and its neighbouring house, Midmar, stone steps set into the roadside wall lead to a well concealed footpath (**A**) which runs between the gardens of the two properties. Initially, this path is very narrow, but when it has climbed beyond the gardens (through thickish bracken in summer) it becomes a pleasant route up the hillside, passing through a copse before coming to a wall above the quarry. Climb over the wall and skirt around the bottom of the field above the quarries to reach a track that goes to Gimmerknowe, a cottage that can be seen on the left. Bear right, go through the gate at the top (**B**) and turn left onto a pleasant track leading below Ship Crag towards woodland. Pass Whinhause (the house formerly called Brae Head) on the left, still climbing.

After Physic Lane joins the route from Thropton on the left the stone wall on that side gradually bends away to the west. A clump of trees is passed on the left — continue straight on along the main track at this point.

Turn to the left at the next opportunity — a major crossways (**C**) — around the shoulder of the hill. A wonderful panorama opens up at this point with the remains of Cartington Castle amidst trees to the left. This dates from the early fourteenth century though its licence to crenellate was granted later, in 1441. A century after this it was described as being 'a good fortresse of two toures and

The River Coquet near Rothbury

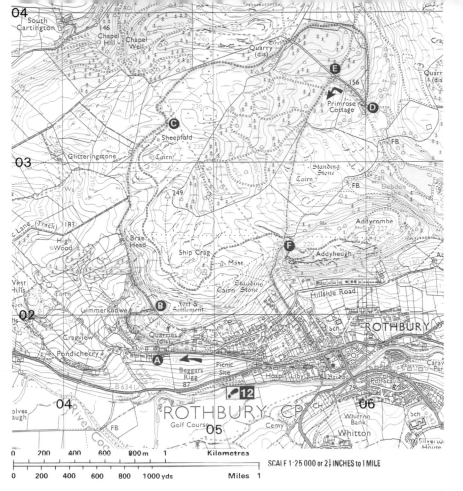

other strange houses'. In 1648 it suffered from being under fire from Parliamentary forces. The siege lasted for just two hours and the castle was left in ruins. In the distance beyond Cartington the long shape of The Cheviot can be identified, with Hedgehope to its right.

A little further and the track arrives at the corner of the timber planting and then descends gently to more woodland. Cross another track, following the sign 'footpath to Primrose Cottage'. This is a delightful section with woods to the right and views down to Debdon on the left. The path dips down to Primrose Cottage (**D**), passing beehives. Turn sharply to the right here, passing through the gate and following a track leading steeply uphill through the wood.

Keep a sharp watch to the left of the track, looking for a stile (**E**) and gate with a signpost to Rothbury. This path threads past pines and beech trees until another footpath sign on the left points to a stile which takes it out of the wood onto the moor again. Head for the radio mast ahead, looking for an ancient parish boundary stone by the wayside as the path threads through the heather,

descending to the bottom of the wood on the left. It crosses another footpath which emerges from the wood (turn right at this point (**F**) if you wish to reach the best viewpoint — the cairn marked on the map). Otherwise continue on the downward path towards Rothbury with the wood on the left. The views to the south, over the town and river to the dark ridge of the Simonside Hills, are truly memorable. These hills, of fell sandstone, have distinctive outlines that have been compared with breaking waves. The outlying summits are Dove Crag to the left and Raven's Heugh to the right. Cross Hillside Road and resume the descent to the town, emerging at its centre.

Here refreshment can be found in a variety of hostelries, or you can continue on the route, passing the National Park Information Centre and the church on the left. There is a footpath leading down steps to the riverside walk by the lamp-post beyond the church (a graveyard is on the right). Turn right onto the riverside walk and having passed the gardens of the County Hotel look for a path on the right which leads up to the picnic site starting point.

13 Bolam Lake and Shaftoe Crags

Start: Bolam Lake Country Park, near Belsay

Distance: 6 miles (9.5 km)

Approximate time: 3 hours

Parking: Northern car park, Bolam Lake Country Park

Refreshments: None

Ordnance Survey maps: Landranger 81 (Alnwick & Morpeth) and Pathfinder 523, NZ 08/18 (Morpeth West)

General description This is a nicely balanced walk with field paths through pastoral countryside for half the distance, and a moorland section leading to a famous viewpoint which overlooks much of Northumberland. Bolam Lake is a favourite 100-acre beauty spot which is always busy on summer weekends. It was created in the nineteenth century by John Dobson, a Newcastle architect who turned the 'splashy lands' here into a beautifully landscaped lake.

Bolam church, with its Saxon tower dating from 960, is one of the ecclesiastical treasures of the county, though the village it served has largely vanished. It became deserted in the sixteenth century even though it had previously boasted a market and fair as well as 200 houses.

From the Warden's office walk down to the lake, peaceful early in the morning and specially beautiful in early summer when the rhododendrons are in bloom. Turn left along a path which leads round the eastern side of the lake close to the road. At the end of the causeway the path ends and for a few yards you have to walk on the road.

At the road junction cross straight over the Belsay road to the farmyard entrance of Bolam Low House (**A**). Pass through this and the white gate immediately on the left. Cross the paddock to a stile in the opposite corner and follow the left side of the next field down to a footbridge. After this keep the fence on the left through the next field and after the gate carry straight on between the plantings of new trees towards the corner of the wood by Shortflatt Tower – a fourteenth-century pele tower incorporated into a later structure. Cross the bridge and track and follow the southern and western sides of a meadow, reaching a driveway which takes a more direct line but is not a right of way. Go over this to climb a stile (**B**) and cross a

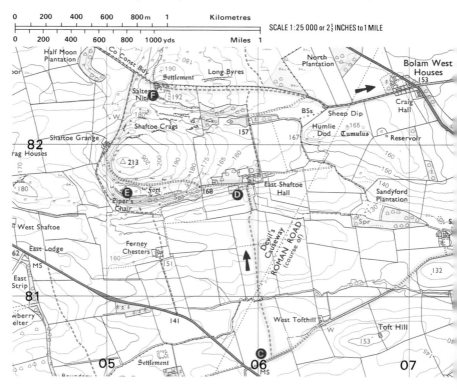

The Piper's Chair

footbridge. Now head for the farm buildings on the far side of the next field and before reaching them join a metalled track to pass Sandyford on the right.

The track crosses a lovely long meadow with delightful open views of the surrounding countryside on the right. Toft Hill blocks the view to the south. Further on, after a bridge and a gate, the lane is fenced as many hedges have vanished. Look for the course of the Devil's Causeway crossing fields to the right after West Tofthill, a modern dwelling.

Before reaching the main road look for a path on the right (**C**) which is a crop divider, heading straight for the large house near the

top of the hill to the north (East Shaftoe Hall). The path crosses two more fields (and the Roman road, though it is difficult to say where) before dipping down to cross a stream where there is a stile and footbridge before climbing up the side of another meadow to the hall. There is an impressive walled garden to the left.

On reaching the drive at the front of the hall (**D**) turn left and pass estate cottages on the right before the track passes through a gate to climb up onto moorland. Remarkably, the track is paved in Roman style at this point, probably the result of a landowner's magnanimity in keeping his workforce employed during the agricultural depression of the last century.

There is a fine view to the south from the rocks (the Piper's Chair) to the left of the track (**E**). A rare breed of small sheep (which might well be mistaken for goats) often shelter behind the weathered crags. Having enjoyed this view it is also worth climbing to the triangulation pillar on the other side of the track to enjoy an even wider vista.

Descend to the track again, which becomes a footpath after Shaftoe Grange, following the wall towards Salters Nick (**F**), a mini-canyon which would be the ideal place for an ambush. This is reached after the wall meets with another and the path turns eastwards.

After the Nick pass through a gate and continue to follow the wall on the left. Almost imperceptibly you pass off the moor and into a large meadow, at the end of which is a rough metalled track leading to Bolam West Houses. Turn right here onto the road and continue along it until a large blue car park sign appears announcing the western parking area of Bolam Lake Country Park.

Enter into the country park here (**G**) and cross the car park to find a long timber boardwalk which takes the path to the northern shore of the lake. If you are here at a quiet time of day you may catch a glimpse of a red squirrel. This is one of its last refuges and it serves as the country park emblem. Roe deer, badgers, and foxes are amongst the other animals which live here.

Continue eastwards along the northern shore to return to the starting point. However, there is an alternative route for those wishing to avoid a quarter of a mile of road walking. The country park boundary is opposite the turn to Sandyford and it can be entered by turning left here. Although there is a maze of small paths in this area of woodland and only instinct will guide you in the correct direction, it would be difficult to become completely lost with the road and the lake so close at hand. Ideally you will head east, finding, after a short while, the lake to your right.

14 Cauldron Snout

Start:	Langdon Beck
Distance:	6 ½ miles (10.5 km)
Approximate time:	3 ½ hours
Parking:	At the point where the Cauldron Snout footpath leaves Langdon Beck to Cow Green Reservoir road, beyond the track to Widdy Bank Farm
Refreshments:	Langdon Beck Hotel is ½ mile (0.75 km) from the starting point and in season Widdybank Farm also provides refreshments
Ordnance Survey maps:	Landrangers 91 (Appleby-in-Westmorland) and 92 (Barnard Castle), Outdoor Leisure 31 (Teesdale)

General description *There is easy walking for the greater part of this route but great care must be taken on the section below Falcon Clints, where, as the name suggests, the path is through a scatter of boulders and loose stone. Arrival below the waterfall is a wonderful reward for the scramble and this must be the most satisfying way to visit Cauldron Snout, at its most impressive after a night of heavy rain. Be careful of the many old mine shafts in the area, some of which may still be open and thus attractive to dogs or children who stray from the path.*

The path follows the track which twists and turns towards white-painted Widdy Bank Farm (**A**). The garden grows brave flowers and vegetables for such a windswept spot (Upper Teesdale has 20.8 days of snow in an average January and its summer temperatures are akin to those of Reykjavik). Teas and snacks may be obtained from the farm in season. Go through the farmyard and a meadow to join a riverside track which passes by an Upper Teesdale Nature Reserve noticeboard. Perhaps in recognition of this the numerous grouse seem ridiculously tame.

The walking on this stretch (Holmwath) is perfect. Springy grass underfoot and grand scenery all about. All too soon, however, the terrain changes as the path becomes narrow and closer to the river. Rocks and boulders slow progress though long runs of slatted boards give relief. These allow the grass to reinstate itself in boggy places where the path has become eroded. No expense has been spared in covering the path across the

marshy land of Lingy Holm (**B**) with these walkways.

Take great care over the huge boulders as the riverside path nears the meeting of the Maize Beck with the Tees. Stone-built cattle-shelters overlook the two streams. The noise of the waterfall can now be clearly heard, and if there has been recent rain its appearance is no anti-climax. Because you are so close to its turbulent waters the spectacle is even more impressive than High Force. The waterfall (**C**) owes its existence to a geological event which took place 295 million years ago — the formation of the Great Whin Sill. A great volcanic upsurge of molten quartz dolerite intruded into the various strata lying above, completely changing the composition of the various rocks as it flowed sideways and upwards, and creating the

whinstone crag over which the water cascades. The characteristic six-sided blocks which can be seen as you climb up the rocks by the side of the waterfall were formed by the rapid cooling of the dolerite intrusion into a crystalline form.

The concrete dam comes into view near the top. There is a dizzy view down from here — not enjoyable by those who suffer from vertigo.

Join the road leading to Birkdale and turn right, thus leaving the Pennine Way. You will soon be walking by the shore of the Cow Green Reservoir. The numbered posts that you see are the various stops on the Nature Conservancy's Widdybank Fell Nature Trail. A booklet on this may be bought at the car park at Cow Green.

Another by-product of the Whin Sill metamorphosis was the creation of sugar limestone. This supports a remarkable range of plants, among them the spring gentian. This is its only habitat in mainland Britain.

A further result of the igneous intrusion was the creation of minerals, the most valuable being barytes and lead. Cow Green was one of a number of mines which flourished here until about the turn of the century. Reminders of the mining industry are still to be seen on the landscape here and on other parts of Teesdale and Alston Moor.

When the path divides (**D**) take the fork to the right to join the road from Cow Green Reservoir car park. It is about two miles (3.25 km) back to the starting point from here along the road. This is enjoyable as the scenery remains superb and there are no demanding gradients.

15 Egglestone Abbey, Paradise and the Meeting of the Waters

Start:	Egglestone Abbey, near Barnard Castle
Distance:	7 miles (11.25 km)
Approximate time:	3 hours
Parking:	Car park by abbey ruins
Refreshments:	Pub at Whorlton
Ordnance Survey maps:	Landranger 92 (Barnard Castle), Outdoor Leisure 31 (Teesdale), and Pathfinder 599, NZ 01/11 (Barnard Castle & Gainford)

General description *This is a straight-forward walk beside the River Tees as it flows majestically by crags and rocks through woodland and farmland. There are monastic ruins, an ancient tower and a grand country house along the route, and on every inch of the path you are treading in the footsteps of great painters and writers from the Romantic age.*

Leave the car park at Egglestone Abbey and head back down the access road beside the ruins. The abbey was built in a charming position overlooking the Tees where it is joined by the waters of the Thorsgill Beck. It was a Premonstratensian foundation of the late twelfth century, colonised by the monks from Easby Abbey near Richmond. After the dissolution it was converted into a manor house, but enough of its fabric survives to make this still a holy spot.

After the cattle-grid turn right along Abbey Lane, cross the road at Abbey Bridge and go through the gate into the wood where the footpath sign points to the Meeting of the Waters and Whorlton (**A**). The newly made path zigzags down to the river which here flows swiftly through a long limestone gorge, a popular place for white-water canoeists. Follow the path down the gorge with crags rearing up on either side, then cross the stepping stones at Manyfold Beck and climb the steep steps into the field high above the river. Stay close beside the fence to the left and climb the sturdy wooden stile into Paradise, the delightful name of this ancient woodland. In addition to commonplace north country broadleafed trees, you will see limes, yews and Spanish chestnuts growing here.

Follow the path as it meanders through Paradise, then go through the gate and turn left into Mortham Lane (**B**).

Across parkland to the right there are glimpses of Rokeby Hall, a grand country house built in 1731 by Sir Thomas Robinson, a noted amateur architect and patron of the arts. Sir Walter Scott stayed there on working holidays to write his novels and poetry, and the painters Turner and Cotman recorded all of Teesdale's beauty spots while based at Rokeby. One of Turner's greatest landscapes is of the Meeting of the Waters, where the turbulent waters of the Greta join the broader Tees (**C**). This scene remained unchanged from Turner's visit until the floods caused by the hurricane in October 1987 rearranged the bedrock in an awesome demonstration of elemental force.

Follow the lane right and then turn left over Dairy Bridge; look down into the peat-brown waters of the Greta rushing through the narrow limestone gorge. At the cattle-grid there is a helpful footpath map on the gate. Follow the drive, turning right up the hill to Mortham Tower, originally a fourteenth-century pele or tower house built to protect against border raiders. Turn left off the drive (**D**) and take the grassy path along the ridge, crossing three stiles standing beside field

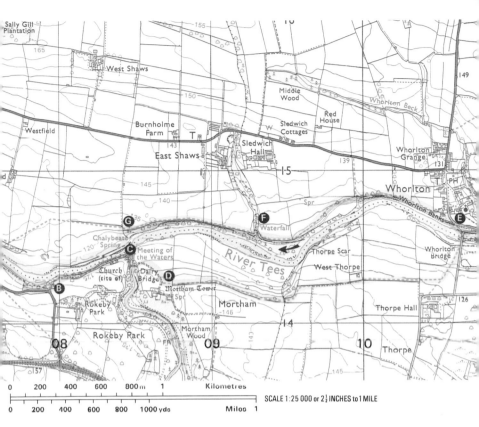

SCALE 1:25 000 or 2½ INCHES to 1 MILE

gates and keeping the neat hedge on the right. There are cultivation terraces in the broad fields running down to the river, with prominent sandstone cliffs beyond. There are several large pinkish boulders beside the path – these are glacial erratics of Shap granite transported here from the Lake District by glaciers in the last Ice Age.

Cross the cartbridge and bear left round the fence beside the wood; then turn right to walk the headland path alongside the wall past the ruins of West Thorpe. This is rich arable farmland, and the transition from pasture to plough marks the boundary between hill farming and lowland farming. Go through the metal field gate, then bear left to the stile in the roadside wall some fifty paces from the southern end of Whorlton Bridge. Cross the bridge, a remarkable suspension design built in 1831, and by the toll cottage on the north bank turn left to climb up the very long flight of steps. At the top a footpath sign points left, but if you are in need of refreshment at this point you must divert up the road to the Bridge Inn which overlooks the village green.

Back at the footpath sign (E), follow the grassy path back updale with the Tees always in sight to your left. There are numerous stiles and gates, but the route is straight-forward until Sledwich Gill (F). Here there is a tricky descent down to bedrock stepping stones across the beck which can be slippery at all times of the year. A steep ascent follows to more stiles and gates. Beyond the last stile at the western end of Sledwich Wood (G) the public footpath bears away to the right but the preferred route to which the right of way is intended to be transferred zigzags steeply down to the Meeting of the Waters. This is the view which Turner painted, complete with an angler in the foreground near the chalybeate spring – look for the red iron-stains on the surrounding bedrock.

Walk along beside the ruined wall, go through the gate, and then bear left to the riverbank. Look out here for waterfowl, as this stretch of the Tees is home to a variety of ducks. Herons and dippers also live here, and you may even catch the electric-blue flash of a kingfisher. Go on along the riverbank and pass through the gate in the corner of the field to follow the woodland path back into the gorge. Abbey Bridge is seen ahead, a single lofty arch built in 1773 vaulting from crag to crag with embattled parapets above and the cascading river beneath. Turn left to cross the busy bridge, then right, and finally fork left to return to the abbey.

16 Hadrian's Wall at Walltown and Thirlwall Castle

General description This section of Hadrian's Wall is one of the most spectacular, but is seldom as crowded as those further east. After a 2-mile (3.25 km) walk along the wall a return is made by the vallum, the defensive ditch built to the south of the wall which also provided an easy corridor of communication along its length. The longer walk provides an opportunity to appreciate the wall from an attacker's viewpoint and to see a later defensive structure, the medieval Thirlwall Castle. If the weather has been wet take care in using the stepping-stones across the Tipalt Burn.

Start:	Walltown, to north of Military Road (B6318), 1 mile (1.5 km) east of Greenhead
Distance:	7 ½ miles (12 km). Shorter version) 4 ½ miles (7.25 km)
Approximate time:	4 hours (2 ½ hours for shorter version)
Parking:	National Park car park just before Walltown Farm
Refreshments:	Tearoom at Holmhead, opposite Thirlwall Castle
Ordnance Survey maps:	Landrangers 86 (Haltwhistle, Bewcastle & Alston) and 87 (Hexham & Haltwhistle), Pathfinder 546, NY 66/76 (Haltwhistle & Gilsland)

From the parking space take the path up to Hadrian's Wall which here crosses the Nine Nicks of Thirlwall, though only five 'nicks' are to be seen today. They are short gaps in the crag which the Romans had to overcome in building their wall. Four have been lost because of quarrying. Although the route of the walk lies eastwards it is worth climbing the short length to the west (**A**) to take in the magnificent view over the quarry towards the hills of Cumbria. As we shall see on the last lap of the walk, the County Council are in the process of reclaiming Walltown Quarry, which was an important source of whinstone for road surfaces until 1978.

Turn back eastwards following the wall:

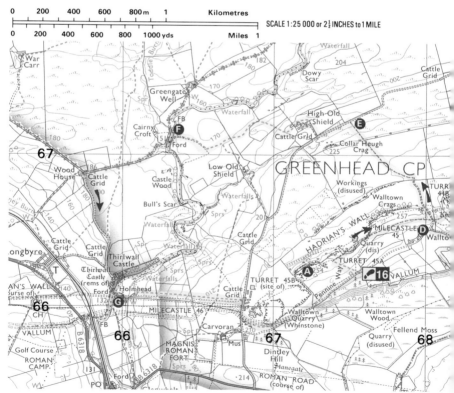

Walltown Crags

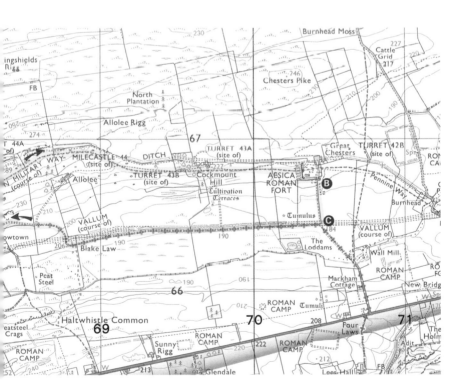

this short section incorporates up to fourteen courses of original stonework making it one of the best-preserved stretches. Chives and other medicinal herbs flourish here and it may be that these derive from seeds sown by legionaries. Because of this it was a location much frequented by Elizabethan herbalists. The fabric of the wall deteriorates after the remains of Turret 45A (which was unusual in having been built before the wall itself). The turrets were spaced between the larger milecastles, about a third of a Roman mile apart. It seems most likely that they were primarily look-out posts, being manned by detachments from the milecastles.

The descent to Walltown Nick is steep, as is the climb on the other side. The wall follows the rising and falling ground eastwards like a switchback and makes for energetic walking. Little of its fabric survives above ground. It passes Allolee, plunging down before climbing steeply up to the site of Milecastle 44 on the other side. These small forts were set at intervals of a Roman mile along the wall and provided access through the wall as well as accommodation for a small platoon of soldiers.

There is a more gentle descent to the next farmstead, Cockmount Hill, which is sheltered by a planting of conifers. The path passes through the trees and past the front of the house to reach the giant cattle-sheds at

Great Chesters where there was an important Roman command centre — the fort known as Aesica. The most interesting feature of Aesica is at its centre surrounded by a fence. This is the entry to the vaulted underground strongroom of the garrison which held the soldiers' pay. The fort also had its own granary and shrines as well as administrative buildings, while outside the perimeter, in the field to the east, were situated the bath house, steam room and latrines. The water to service this complex, built in AD 128, was brought by aqueduct from a stream more than 2 miles (3.25 km) away. However, to maintain the correct rate of flow the aqueduct was 6 miles (9.5 km) long and a remarkable feat of engineering.

Turn right here (**B**) away from the farm down its drive, and then right again (**C**) to follow the course of the vallum along an unclassified county road. Vallum is the Latin for 'wall', but in this instance it is a defensive ditch about 130 feet (40 m) wide. The mistake is said to have originated from the writings of the Venerable Bede, and no-one subsequently corrected it. The vallum marked the beginning of the military zone but there were causeways across it guarded by gates which gave access to milecastles.

The vallum gives an excellent view of Hadrian's Wall from the south — even from this aspect it looks formidable. The track

Thirlwall Castle

leaves the vallum at Blake Law and joins with the drive from Allolee. It crosses a cattle-grid and passes an old quarry-working. King Arthur's Well, a hill fort from pre-Roman times, is seen ahead, to the right.

For the shorter walk, follow the road back past Walltown Farm to the starting point.

Turn to the right just before the farm (**D**), climbing up to the wall again at the declivity below King Arthur's Well.

From here the path heads north-west over rather soggy ground along what seems an ancient paved way. Pass through a muddy gateway and fork left on what looks suspiciously like a sheep track. The road can soon be seen in the distance on the right. Head for the stone wall and from here look for a stile over the next wall just to the right of the roof of High Old Shield (binoculars would come in handy!)

Cross this stile and a small footbridge to reach the road (**E**) and turn left. Walk up the drive of High Old Shield and pass to the right of the house and round the back of it through two farmyard gates so that you emerge on the west side of the house. Now head for the gate in the stone wall at the bottom of the field. Go through this and make for the white cottage with three pine trees. There is a ladder-stile over the wall ahead; after this, descend through the next meadow, still heading for Cairny Croft. The Tipalt Burn (**F**) lies between you and the road and has to be crossed by stepping-stones, easy enough in dry spells but hazardous if it is in spate.

Turn left onto the road. There is a lovely view back as it climbs steadily uphill. Turn left at the junction and descend to Thirlwall Castle, taking the rough farm track by the ruins. The castle was built of stone taken from Hadrian's Wall which accounts for there being little trace of the wall above ground in the vicinity. Edward I is supposed to have slept at Thirlwall in 1306 though other accounts give the date of its completion forty years later. Although it was lived in until the eighteenth century, it was already delapidated in 1542. Legend has it that a ghostly dwarf guards the castle's treasure — a table made of solid gold. The track leads down to the Tipalt Burn which is crossed this time by a footbridge (**G**) at a delightful spot (Holmhead) where there is a cottage overlooking the stream which provides refreshments for hikers (this is a section of the Pennine Way).

Bear left up the steep slope to reach the vallum. This is a magnificent stretch which climbs steeply up the hill. Turn right at the lane to pass the newly landscaped Walltown Quarry, then left onto the footpath along its edge to return to the start of the walk.

17 Humbleton Burn, Gains Law and Commonburn

Start:	Humbleton Burn picnic area
Distance:	7 miles (11.25 km)
Approximate time:	3 hours
Parking:	Humbleton Burn picnic area where Common Road, Wooler, crosses the burn
Refreshments:	Pubs and cafés in Wooler
Ordnance Survey maps:	Landrangers 74 (Kelso) and 75 (Berwick-on-Tweed), Pathfinder 745, NT 82/92 (The Cheviots, North)

General description The outward part of this route provides truly magnificent scenery so be sure to choose a day when visibility is good. There are grand views towards Scotland, and the Northumberland coast is well seen with Holy Island and Bamburgh Castle distinctive landmarks. Good visibility is also important in the navigation of the westernmost section where landmarks are few. The return is on a good track from Commonburn House, passing through stretches of forest.

Refer to map overleaf.

Cross the bridge and take the bridleway to the right signposted to Humbleton. This follows the stream for a few yards and then forks to the left up the hill. You may pause to recover breath at the first gate on a seat thoughtfully provided. The climb continues beyond the gate where you keep straight on following the blue bridleway arrow. On the right the view opens up over the coastal plain (the white steeple beyond Doddington clearly visible).

Go through the gate (**A**) by the British Rail van which has been put out to grass. Turn to the left and then immediately right on a grassy track which climbs steadily round the flank of Coldberry Hill. The coastline is visible beyond Humbleton Hill which has an imposing prehistoric fort with stone ramparts on the summit and lynchets or medieval cultivation terraces on its eastern flank. The summits of the Cheviots appear massively spectacular to the left of the track.

Pass through two gates: beyond the second there is a cairn with a post bearing a cluster of yellow footpath arrows. Keep straight on along the track to Gains Law. When the path levels out there are grand views into Scotland. Scald Hill lies ahead while there is a gully to the left. On the right Monday Cleugh is a rocky, dry valley which separates Gains Law from Harehope Hill, just to the north. In 1402 this was the scene of a bloody encounter when Henry Percy (Hotspur of Shakespeare's history plays) ambushed a Scottish raiding party led by Douglas. Hotspur's archers fired their arrows at the Scots hiding above them on Humbleton Hill and, according to a contemporary account, left them looking like hedgehogs. Further fighting took place on the other side of the main road between Akeld and Humbleton where there is a field called Red Rigg, a name (with that of the battle stone close by) which commemorates the slaughter. In the opening scene of *King Henry IV Part 1*, the King is told of Hotspur's success in this battle. A little way to the north-west of this battlefield is the site of an even greater conflict, Flodden Field, where the English comprehensively routed the Scots in 1513.

Turn left just before the next gate to reach a stile (**B**) over the fence. The path, having thus left the track, cuts across the heathery expanse of Black Law heading towards the bulk of The Cheviot. It rejoins the other path at the corner of the wall and continues alongside it until it reaches a gate. Here, cross to the right-hand side of the wall. Commonburn House can now be seen ahead though the right of way dictates a detour away from the direct route.

At the end of the wall (**C**) bear right to follow a faint path which heads to the right of a clump of trees on the hillside (there is a new planting to the right of this, on the other side of the small valley). A useful cairn is a guide across boggy ground to a gate between the two plantings. It is easy to appreciate that this was treacherous ground in days before modern drainage. Yeavering Bell, the summit to the north, is crowned with the largest hill fort of the Borders, a stone rampart enclosing an area of 17 acres (6.9 ha) which probably contained at least 130 timber huts. It dates from *c*. 500 BC. Closer to the right is Tom Tallon's Crag: no-one knows who this character was or what befell him to give this outcrop his name, though a tumulus once stood nearby.

Make for the gate (and ladder) on the skyline ahead (**D**) and having crossed this boundary keep straight ahead over featureless moor until you come to another path where the heather seems to have been checked. Turn left here (**E**), then scan the skyline to the south for another ladder over the wall crossed earlier. The Cheviot looms directly behind it. Make for this ladder when you spot it. From here a distinct track leads down to Commonburn House.

Bear off to the left before the farm to join the track running directly eastwards from the farm. It is a relief to walk on a solid surface, and the road passes through various forestry plantings before randomly placed picnic tables warn of approaching civilisation. Within the hour from Commonburn you will be back at Humbleton Burn picnic area.

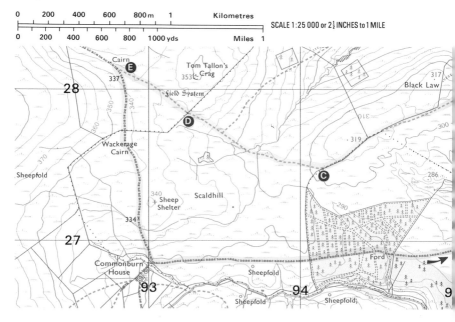

SCALE 1:25 000 or 2½ INCHES to 1 MILE

The vista from Coldberry Hill

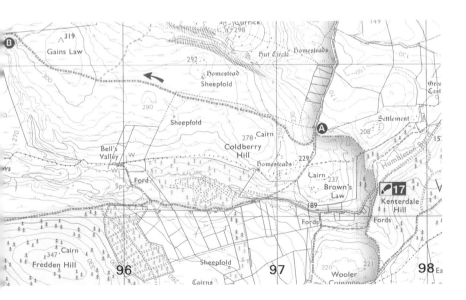

18 Wolsingham and the Weardale Way

Start: Wolsingham

Distance: 7 ½ miles (12 km)

Approximate time: 3 hours

Parking: Lay-by on the Hamsterley Road at Wear Bank, opposite the drive to Ashes Farm (Ashes House on map). The lay-by is situated below power cables spanning the road at this point

Refreshments: Pubs at Wolsingham and Frosterley

Ordnance Survey maps: Landranger 92 (Barnard Castle) and Outdoor Leisure 31 (Teesdale)

General description *Too often Weardale is neglected in favour of the more famous Teesdale. This walk may stimulate an interest in its delightful countryside. There are no severe gradients in this stroll, which passes through the pastures of the valley to climb to the grouse moor above. There are spectacular views along and over Weardale from the long-distance path — the Weardale Way — which follows the top of the valley at this point. The return is made on the path which follows the south bank of the river.*

Cross the road to the track to Ashes Farm opposite (there is no waymark). Wolsingham looks very picturesque from this track. It dips down to cross a stream: Ashes Farm is on the right. Beyond, it continues as a good field track to pass through the farmyard at Towdy Potts.

Turn left after the farmyard (**A**) through a gate onto another equally pleasing field track. On the right a line of thorn trees shows that the hedgerow is ancient. Frosterley can be seen in the distance beyond them. The track ends at a gap in a stone wall (**B**) with electric lines overhead. Turn left here to follow the wall up the hill towards the small wood at the top.

The footpath swings away eastwards at the bottom of the plantation to meet with a bridleway at a small gate in the stone wall on the left. Do not go through this but turn right and climb up through a small patch of gorse to reach the gate at the top of the field by the wood (**C**).

Go through the gate and turn right onto the broad track that winds over the moor following the wall that divides it from the

pastures below. There are splendid views over Weardale — Stanhope can be seen in the distance. Far ahead, on the skyline, is a clump of trees (known locally as the Elephant Trees). One field before them, go through the gate on the right (**D**) and descend towards Frosterley with the wall on the right.

Almost immediately a circular sheepfold with fir trees growing within its walls comes into view below: pass to the right of this, continuing to follow the wall on the right. Having gone through the gate at the bottom of this field you pass another circular sheepfold, this time on the right. The path joins with a track which curves round the hill to a gate in the lower left corner of the field. The Frosterley quarries are in sight below as the track bears off to the right away from the village, following the wall on the left. Keep following the track when it turns to the left through a red gate to reach the farm at West

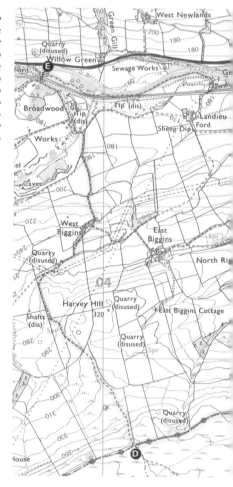

Biggins. Do not take the track to the right which leaves the farmyard, but continue down to cross a bridge. Fork left before Broadwood to reach (and cross) a level-crossing.

If you wish to seek refreshment in Frosterley carry on over the bridge and turn left along a byway before the main road for a quiet route to the village. Otherwise, turn right (E) before the bridge onto a riverside path.

Keeping strictly to the path cross the meadow to a footbridge over the Bollihope Burn which leads into a short stretch of woodland close to the river.

The footpath continues along the riverbank as it skirts a vast array of caravans on the right. Just before the end of the site the path bends away from the river, passing the managerial bungalow, and then turns left to follow a tarmac driveway, with the railway close to the right.

When the drive bears off to the left to cross the bridge over the Wear, keep straight on along a narrow footpath with the river close to the left. The sound of rushing water heralds a weir, opposite which the path goes through a small gate, across a footbridge and into a long narrow meadow. Keep to the right side of this, close to the railway. The walking is very pleasant here on sheep-cropped turf as it is through a second, even longer, meadow.

The river is now some distance to the left. Go over another footbridge into a third narrow meadow, still keeping to the railway side (do not head for the tempting white gate at the end).

Soon you can see the road bridge over the railway ahead; go up the steps to the road and turn right. The brief climb that follows to return to the starting place is the most taxing that is encountered on this route.

SCALE 1:25 000 or 2½ INCHES to 1 MILE

19 Windy Gyle

Start:	Near Windyhaugh about 6 miles (9.5 km) upstream from Alwinton
Distance:	7 miles (11.25 km)
Approximate time:	4½ hours
Parking:	Where Rowhope Burn joins the River Coquet just north-west of Windyhaugh
Refreshments:	None
Ordnance Survey maps:	Landranger 80 (Cheviot Hills & Kielder Forest), and Pathfinder 487, NT 81/91 (Cheviot Hills, Central)

Looking into Scotland from Russell's Cairn

General description *For some reason gloomy names have been attached to many of the features encountered on this walk – Dreary Sike, The Slime, Foul Step – yet this should put no-one off from experiencing the splendour of Windy Gyle. The summit, Russell's Cairn, is an incomparable viewpoint on a fine day (and this is not a route to be undertaken in adverse conditions). The walk up to this part of the Pennine Way has relatively easy gradients even though they seem to go on for a long way. Much of the surrounding land serves as a Ministry of Defence Dry Training Area, so be careful not to stray from the authorised paths.*

Windyhaugh is notable on the long cul-de-sac up the Coquetdale Valley for having both a school and a telephone box. Just under a mile from the hamlet the road crosses the bridge over the Rowhope Burn – the starting point.

Take the asphalted track which runs up the valley alongside the burn. At Rowhope Farm, the stream divides and the track follows the Trows Burn, the eastern tributary, up to the farmhouse which takes its name from this watercourse. After the house take the left-hand track (**A**) which goes through a ford – though there is also a footbridge.

There follows a steep climb up to Trows Law, one of the few testing gradients on the route. On days when the army is not firing the silence up here is overwhelming – you will be unfortunate indeed if you hear a motor vehicle in the next three hours or so. The crows or 'hoodies' – birds hated by shepherds – fly in joyful exuberance and the grass is springy underfoot. As you climb the view becomes ever more spectacular behind you – a good excuse for pausing to catch breath. An army noticeboard reminds walkers that this is an army training area. Do not pick up any strange objects. Continue on the track, even though this becomes less distinct. A grand array of summits comes into view ahead.

The track winds up to another military noticeboard (**B**). Bear to the left here and continue climbing, not forgetting to look back. At the top you come to a fence with a stile which leads to a cairn (**C**) and triangulation pillar. This is Russell's Cairn which bestrides the border between England and Scotland and is one of Britain's classic viewpoints. The actual cairn is prehistoric even though it takes its name from Lord Francis Russell, who was killed here in 1585 at the side of his father-in-law, Sir John Forster, the Warden of the Middle Marches, during a Wardens' Tryst or Meeting. There is said to have been a drovers' inn and even a cockpit up here at one time. The view extends far into the lowlands of Scotland (Sir Walter Scott's Eildon Hills being easily identified) while in other directions the soft curves of the Cheviot landscape stretch to a lonely infinity.

Russell's Cairn is on the route of the Pennine Way, which we now follow westwards with the fence on the left. It is a well used path along the ridge. The Way is probably the most famous of Britain's long distance footpaths. The route was first proposed in 1935 but was not opened until thirty years later. The original aim of the 250-mile route – to link 'the high places of solitude' – makes it as successful an expedition today as it was in the days of its conception. At the bottom of a dip climb a stile over the fence which divides here (**D**): Windy Rigg is to the right, on the left are the headwaters of the various tributaries of the Rowhope Burn which seem to have their origins in the morass known as Foul Step. Our route follows the Pennine Way in cutting a corner here, leaving the fence to dip into boggy Foulstep Sike and climbing up the steep western side. There is a similar obstacle at Richard's Cleugh.

When this path meets the fence again, at a corner (**E**), leave the Pennine Way by taking the track straight ahead towards an army noticeboard. This is a fine ridge walk with a steep drop on the right to Easthope Burn. The path follows a well worn gulley over Black Braes and then descends before climbing Swineside Law.

The views are a compensation for the climb which is the last on this route. Follow the fence on the most-used path down from here. This is The Street, an ancient drovers' way which eventually reaches the bridge over the Rowhope Burn — the starting point of the walk where one mystery remains. Close to the stream there is a signboard looking like a footpath indicator, however, it bears the legend 'Georgius 860115'. It is easy to muse on the reasons for this being here for the entire length of the drive home.

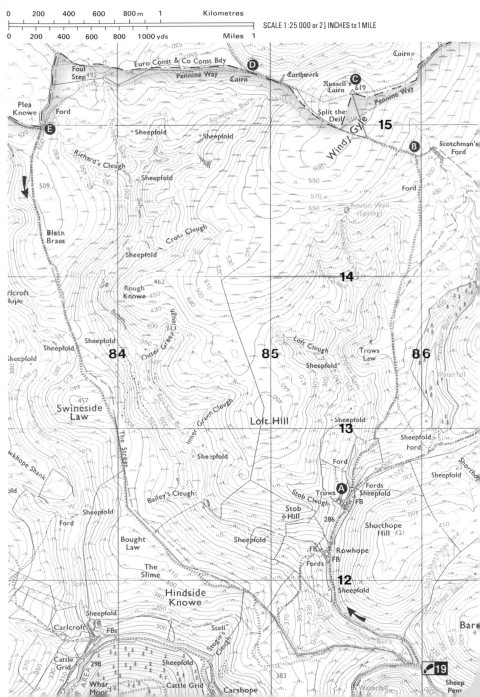

20 Waskerley Way

Start:	Waskerley
Distance:	7½ miles (12 km).
	Shorter version
	5½ miles (8.75 km)
Approximate time:	4 hours (3 hours for
	shorter version)
Parking:	Picnic site at Waskerley
Refreshments:	Pubs at Castleside
Ordnance Survey	Landrangers 87
maps:	(Hexham &
	Haltwhistle) and 88
	(Tyneside & Durham),
	Pathfinder 571,
	NZ 04/14 (Lanchester)

General description The trackbeds of disused railways provide many excellent walks in County Durham: this route utilises a section of one of the oldest of these. Originally built in 1834 to transport limestone and iron ore from Weardale to Consett, it was later owned by that most famous of railway companies, the Stockton and Darlington. The return from Castleside passes through a variety of terrain. Much of it is on field paths, but quiet lanes, moorland and woodland tracks are used as well. A shorter version is also offered.

It seems incredible today that the lofty, remote moorland hamlet of Waskerley was once a busy railway centre, having a loco shed which housed six engines. Only a few buildings survive from its heyday, amongst them the chapel. The line was closed in 1968.

Leave the picnic site and turn left along the old railway track passing what could have been the engine shed (with heavily buttressed walls) and the chapel. There is a wide view beyond: the Cheviots can be seen on a clear day. Waskerley stands at 1,150 feet (350 m) above sea level. There is a planting of conifers in the very broad cutting where once there were sidings. Pass a seat (**A**) thoughtfully sited at an excellent viewpoint and a little further on go through the gate on the left onto the track to Red House, thus cutting off a corner. The Waskerley Way officially goes on to Burnhill Junction where it joined with a later railway going to Crook and Darlington: if you take this longer route you would turn sharply left to reach Red House.

Turn left at Red House onto the Waskerley Way again. On a windy day it may be wise to walk at the bottom of the deep cutting but then you miss the view which you can enjoy from the path along the top. Over to the left is Nanny Mayer's Incline where full trucks loaded with ore or limestone were used to haul empty ones back up to Waskerley. Mrs Mayer kept a pub close by.

The deep cutting is followed by a broad, high embankment fringed with rowans. After a bridge the old course of the line from the incline joins from the left. A little distance after you will come to the White Hall picnic place (**B**) where the road crosses the track. Turn left onto the road here and after 400 yards (366 m) turn right over a stile onto a footpath towards Castleside.

*The shorter version of this route entails following the road (Healeyfield Lane) to rejoin the longer route at Middles Farm (**G**).*

Head to the left of a ruined building to find a gap in the wire fence and then drop to the road at Watergate Burn. Follow the road uphill for a few yards before taking a narrow footpath on the left (**C**) leading to a lovely wooded valley. After this pass through the gate and walk along the edge of the field with a fence on the right. A track leads on past Dene Howl Farm on the right and then climbs up a narrow steep-sided dry valley. This resembles Devon more than Durham.

Turn right at the road (**D**) and descend down a steep and twisty hill to Comb Bridges (look for footpaths to cut off hairpin bends). Timber felling at Comb Bridges has left the steep side of the valley almost naked. Although there has been no replanting, some regeneration is taking place.

Climb up the lane on the other side of the bridge. Soon a ridge is reached – a narrow neck of land with woods dropping away on both sides separating the valley of the River Derwent from that of the Hisehope Burn. Look for the point where a footpath crosses the road (**E**) and take the path on the left which plunges straight down the side of the valley to a footbridge at the bottom. On the other side of the stream, timber operations have obliterated the footpath.

Climb straight up over the rough ground as best you can to the fence at the top. If it is a wooden fence turn to the left to find the point where it joins another wire fence (a wire fence goes up the hillside at right-angles to both). The path climbs on the left side of the ascending fence, bearing to the left through the trees near the top to reach a pair of ancient wicket gates which take the path into a field (**F**).

Cross this field to a red gate by a length of stone wall. Go through this gate and keep the wall, and then a steep bank, on the left through the field. The path is now following a track going towards Middle Horsleyhope.

Pass through the farmyard and walk down the farm track to the road. Cross over this to another farm track leading to Middles Farm (**G**). Note that the official right of way

detours to the right after the stream, rejoining close to the farm. There is little sign of this path on the ground.

After the hairpin bends keep straight on away from the farm towards a clump of pines. Turn right, following the wall on the left. Waskerley comes into view ahead. Keep the wall on the left past three fields until you come to a patched-up gate in this wall (H) with a ruined building beyond. (Was this once Nanny Mayer's pub?) Use this short track to reach the Incline, and climb this interesting relic of a bygone age to reach Waskerley.

21 Blawearie from Cuddy's Knowe

Start:	Cuddy's Knowe, on the moorland road between North Charlton and Chillingham
Distance:	7 ½ miles (12 km)
Approximate time:	4 hours
Parking:	On broad verge of road at Cuddy's Knowe
Refreshments:	None
Ordnance Survey maps:	Landranger 75 (Berwick-upon-Tweed) and Pathfinder 476, NU 02/12 (Chatton & Ellingham)

General description *This is not a walk to be undertaken on a day when visibility is poor. At times there are few landmarks, and these are usually distant. The TV mast is the most useful of these, especially on the return leg which is on a more distinct path than the outward one. The latter often utilises sheep tracks and those made by shooters' vehicles. However, it provides a good challenge in navigation, and takes the walker over wild and unfrequented country.*

The beginning of this walk presents an enigma. Opposite the road to the Sandyford Moor transmitter there is a footpath sign pointing southwards to Eglingham over the tussocky wilderness of Quarryhouse Moor. However, there is no distinct path here and it is probably better to retreat a few yards eastwards towards the footpath to Hagdon to find the semblance of a track made by grouse-shooters' vehicles. Head due south towards the most easterly cairn which has a distinctive pyramid shape.

From the cairn (**A**) continue southwards to reach a gate in a wall. A few yards beyond this the next landmark appears — a small plantation of conifers. Pass to the right of these still heading south: now you should see telephone poles ahead and gradually a gateway comes into view. On the right are the rocky outcrops of Hare Crag. When you come to the track with the telephone poles bear right and go through the gate (**B**).

There are good all-round views from this track which is why a triangulation pillar is sited on a prominence to the right. Just beyond this bear to the right off the track (**C**) and keep the wall on the left as you walk down towards a plantation (the foreground to a grand array of hills beyond with the distinctive whale-like shape of The Cheviot

prominent). The path dips down to a stream: the ford marked on the map is now unusable and a cattlebridge has to be used instead. Follow the fence alongside the stream round to a stone wall and then turn right to climb up by this towards Harehope. Note that the water tower marked on the map at the farm has now gone.

Pass in front of the cottages at Harehope and turn right through the gate (**D**). Go up the track with the wall on the left and pass through the second gate so that now you are climbing with the wall on the right. Confusion could arise here since the shapes of the fields have been recently altered. Where the wall gives way to a wire fence follow the raised bank which is the old wall as marked on the map. The path leaves this as it descends into a valley. There is a very well-concealed pill box guarding it: a path runs past this and continues northwards to meet with a broken-down wall running along the side of the valley. This leads to a stile (**E**) where the path divides. Our way is to the right, a romantic path clearly seen threading up the steep valley past clumps of sessile oak. Note the boulder on the right of the valley, which looks as though it is poised to drop on invaders — one touch being enough to launch it down the slopes.

This is a steady climb: there are posts to mark the route through the bracken. It would be hard to miss the way as this is a well trodden path. Soon the evocative ruins of Blawearie can be seen ahead, though the sight of them is lost when the path leads through a steep gully. Blawearie was occupied until the Second World War when the building was badly damaged during army exercises. It soon became derelict; the small rocky garden to the rear of the farmhouse speaks of the confidence and love of someone who lived in this isolated place many years ago.

Blawearie

Carry on past the ruined farmhouse (**F**) (either path will do when it divides). The main one is a track leading past beehives concealed by a quarry: the honey made from the heather nectar must be delicious. Climb past the tumble of rocks to the top and the TV mast is revealed on the skyline. Although it twists and turns quite a lot the path mainly heads towards the mast and remains distinct even when it drops into small valleys and the landmark is concealed. To make quite certain that the wayfarer keeps to the right path, lines of posts lead through tricky parts. When the path at last meets the road turn right to return to the starting point.

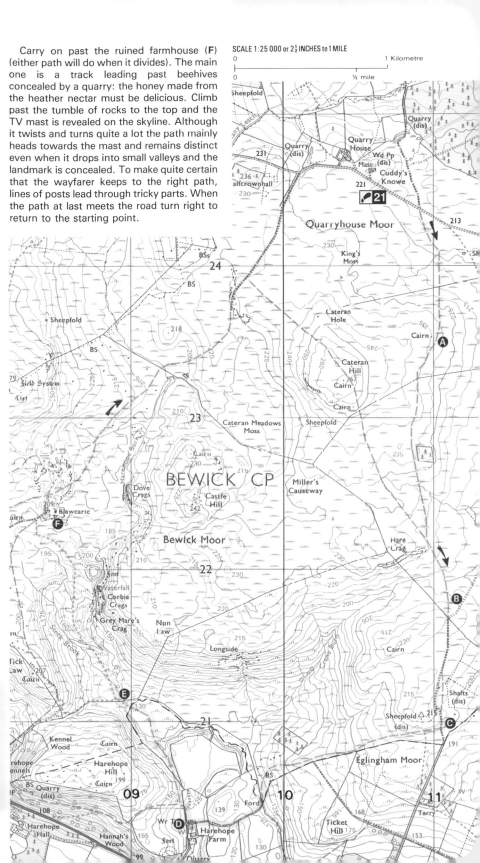

SCALE 1:25 000 or 2½ INCHES to 1 MILE

22 Eccles Cairn and the College Valley

Start:	Hethpool
Distance:	7½ miles (12 km)
Approximate time:	3½ hours
Parking:	There is a small lay-by just before Hethpool on a left-hand bend where the road to Elsdonburn and Trowupburn goes through a gate straight ahead
Refreshments:	None
Ordnance Survey maps:	Landranger 74 (Kelso) and Pathfinder 475, NT 82/92 (Cheviot Hills, North)

General description The College Valley is one of the better kept secrets of the Cheviots. A few permits each day are available from an estate agent in Wooler to motorists who wish to drive up to Mounthooly (it is an easy way to get up to the Pennine Way and The Cheviot) but it is an enjoyable road to walk, and this route explores a lonely tract of country by the border fence as well as the valley itself, which is particularly glorious mantled in autumn colour. Do not attempt this walk unless you are certain of good visibility.

Go through the gate ahead of you on the made-up track labelled to Elsdonburn and Trowupburn. Bear to the right when the road forks, heading towards a farm by the side of a wood. This farm (Elsdonburn) turns out to be a modern bungalow. Pass through the farmyard by walking to the left of the bungalow and follow the yellow waymark through a gate onto a rough track on the open hillside which winds towards plantations. The track dips down to cross Shank's Sike. Go through the gate here and head across the field making for the gate (**A**) at the lower corner of the right-hand planting of conifers.

Go through the gate and turn left so that you are following the left side of the wood with a stream on the right. The small hut on the right is where shepherds would once have lived during lambing. In the distance a path can be seen climbing towards Eccles Cairn. The wood on the left is the home of noisy jays.

At the corner of the wood the path descends to a bridge across the stream. Standing here you should see the first of a series of white-topped posts which mark the

path up to the cairn and are a very useful aid to navigation. From the final post the path bears to the right to reach the viewpoint, Eccles Cairn (**B**).

On a good day this provides a magnificent panorama of the Scottish lowlands. The twin townships of Town Yetholm and Kirk Yetholm are just below: the finishing point of the Pennine Way according to Wainwright, who used to leave a pint 'in salt' here for those stalwarts who managed to complete the route from start to finish. Since his death the measure has been reduced to half a pint, paid for by the brewery. Beyond the Yetholms the Eildon Hills can be seen in the distance, beloved of Sir Walter Scott.

Leave Eccles Cairn on a clear path leading to the south-west to reach the border fence (which is a wall here) and follow this southwards until the Pennine Way joins it through a gate — the signpost is on the Scottish side. Take the track to the left here.

The path skirts the head of a small burn (Maddies Well) and then follows the contours

to reach a fence below Madam Law (**C**). From here the main path leads high up on the left side of the steep valley known as Wide Open. This is too easy. Leave this path early on to descend over rough ground to the bottom of the valley of the Trowup Burn where there is a vague path on the left side. It eventually reaches a gate by a circular sheep pen. Cross the stream here to reach a much broader, grassy path. This leads to more sheep pens which are passed on the left.

A good track leads from these pens to Trowupburn. However, the right of way lies to the right where a broken stile once took the path into the trees, but this route has been overgrown and replaced by another a little further to the south. Climb up with the trees on the left to a point where spruces (Christmas trees) give way to pines with their darker bunches of needles. Here you should just be able to discern a steep path leading into the planting. Although it looks unlikely, it emerges into a broad firebreak with a good path. Now there are spruces on both sides.

This path comes out of the forest above Trowupburn (**D**). Turn to the left on emerging from the conifers to find a well defined path a little lower down which heads towards more trees on the other side of Loft Hill. This is a fine spot to photograph, with the small dwelling of the shepherd providing scale for a vast and lonely landscape.

A gate leads into the next, more extensive, tract of woodland. Pause to look back from here and you may see minute figures on the skyline trudging along the Pennine Way. The gate leads into a firebreak which dips down steeply. Hare Law is the summit on the far side of the College Valley which is slowly revealed. The forest track reaches the valley road above Whitehall. Turn left to follow the road back to Hethpool. There are several lovely places where one can rest by the stream and take in the charm of this hidden beauty spot. The last stretch of the road runs through meadows to reach Hethpool, where the picturesque estate cottages have wonderfully colourful gardens.

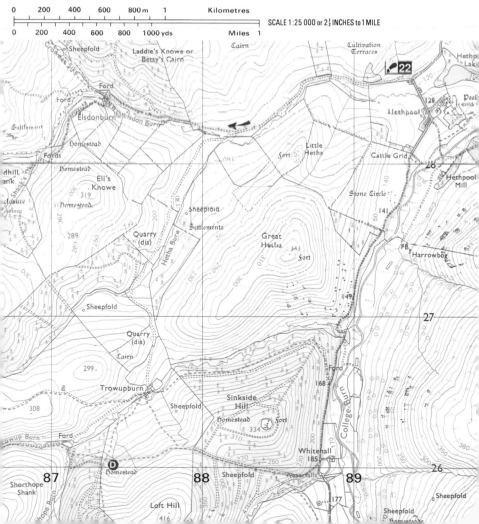

23 Yearning Saddle and Deel's Hill

Start:	Blindburn Bridge, 8 miles (12.75 km) up the Coquet valley from Alwinton
Distance:	7½ miles (12 km)
Approximate time:	4 hours
Parking:	Off the road near Blindburn Bridge
Refreshments:	None
Ordnance Survey maps:	Landranger 80 (Cheviot Hills & Kielder Forest), Pathfinders 486, NT 61/71 (Chesters & Hownam), 487, NY 81/91 (The Cheviot Hills, Central) and 498, NT 60/70 (Catcleugh)

General description *The path by the lovely Blind Burn leads to the mountain shelter on Yearning Saddle, a welcome refuge for those trekking along the border ridge on the Pennine Way. There are seemingly infinite views into Scotland from the northern side of the border ridge. The route then follows the Pennine Way south-westwards across lonely moorland to Brownhart Law (there are excellent views from here too) before heading back to the Coquetdale road over Deel's Hill to Buckham's Bridge. This is an invigorating highland walk without being over-strenuous.*

From the bridge take the path on the west side of the stream, the Blind Burn. Cross the stream over a plank bridge after 300 yards (274 m) and then continue on this side along an excellent path. Dippers and herons will often be seen here. Pass a military sign which warns that this is an uncleared area: the path is safe, however, and the sheep safely graze

On Deel's Hill

on the supposedly hazardous ground on either side. Unfortunately, riders often use this footpath and because of this in places it is in danger of becoming broken up and boggy.

Having crossed a stream coming down

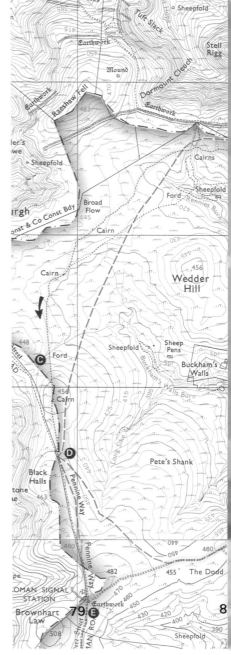

from Gimmermoor Cairns there is a steep climb up to Yearning Hall (**A**), the site of a ruinous croft surrounded by a few weather-beaten pines. The name 'Yearning' is said to derive from the Anglo-Saxon *erne,* a word often given to soaring birds of prey. In the past this area is likely to have been the hunting ground of white-tailed as well as golden eagles, though the latter are rarely seen in the Cheviots today. The white-tailed eagle became extinct in Britain about seventy years ago.

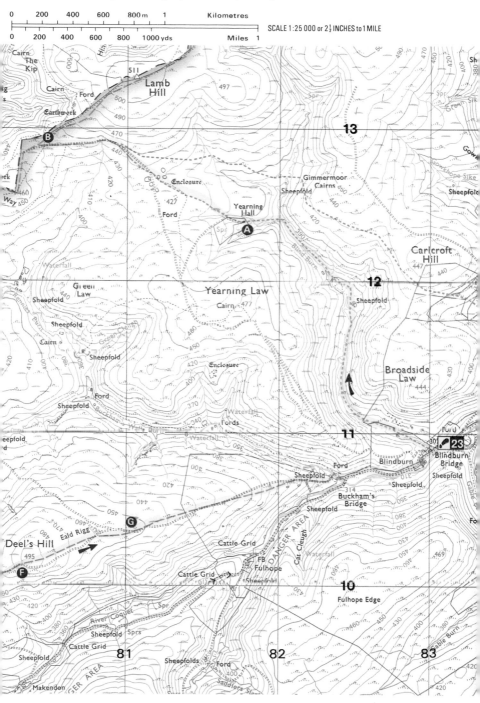

SCALE 1:25 000 or 2½ INCHES to 1 MILE

The climb is less demanding beyond Yearning Hall. The path, such as it is, goes past an ancient circular enclosure and from here a post should be seen ahead which on inspection points ahead to Rennies Burn. Take the other direction offered, turning right here for the border ridge. This proves to be a well used track which winds round to reach the mountain shelter at Yearning Saddle (**B**). There are super views from here if one steps a few yards into Scotland. The Kip is the summit with a pyramid on top. The visitors' book in the shelter shows that Lord Lucan was here recently!

The Pennine Way keeps the fence at a little distance to the right − this section over very bleak moorland may not be very interesting (there are no views into Scotland) but it is typical of much of the long-distance path. A causeway of duckboarding takes it across the head of Buckham's Walls Burn (**C**). After about an hour the path returns to the border ridge at Black Halls: there is a fine view westwards from here. There is no sign of the path on the left (**D**) across the heathery wastes to The Dodd and Deel's Hill, and it is better to continue another half-mile (0.75 km) to Brownhart Law.

There are two footpath-type gates in the fence. At the second of these (**E**) (just after the Way passes through a sort of cutting which gives welcome respite from the wind) take the faint track on the left. (The Pennine Way continues towards a signpost seen in the near distance sited on top of a small hillock, marked on the map as a Roman signal station: the fence changes direction at this point.)

Soon there is a valley on the right and a rounded hill ahead with the forest beyond, slightly to its right. When the track divides (**F**) take the path to the left leading over Deel's Hill. There is a lovely view from the top. The path now heads towards the forest and soon passes a footpath junction (**G**) where the path on the left is waymarked to Buckham's Walls. There is now lovely turf underfoot. A strange standing stone of black rock may be seen on the right before the path reaches the road at Buckham's Bridge. Continue eastwards along it by the infant waters of the Coquet to reach Blindburn Bridge.

The view from the Pennine Way at Black Halls

24 Hartside, Salters Road and High Cantle

Start:	Hartside, 6 miles (9.5 km) west of A697, beyond Powburn and Ingram
Distance:	8 miles (12.75 km)
Approximate time:	4½ hours
Parking:	On the verge of public road before Hartside Farm
Refreshments:	None
Ordnance Survey maps:	Landranger 80 (Cheviot Hills & Kielder Forest) and Pathfinder 487, NT 81/91 (Cheviot Hills, Central)

General description *This walk displays one of the most enjoyable characteristics of the Cheviots — their loneliness. For much of it you have to strain your eyes to see signs of human occupation, if any is visible at all. Some of the way is on vague, heathery tracks made either by sheep or shooting parties. It is wise to take a compass and only try the route on a day of good visibility (in murky weather its wonderful vistas would be wasted in any case)*

Refer to map overleaf.

Take the farm road branching to the left at Hartside which leads to Alnhammoor. The River Breamish is soon on the right forming a foreground for the lovely Cheviot landscape covered by this walk. At Alnhammoor (the dogs make it likely that this is still a shepherd's cottage) cross the bridge, climb to the top of the incline, and turn left before the house on a path which is waymarked as a permissive path. Turn sharply to the right at the end of this short path (**A**) to pass behind the farmhouse.

The Shank Burn is now on the left. Keep to the lower path and cross the fence at a stile bearing a footpath waymark just beyond a stell (round sheepfold). Cross a streamlet (the Rowhope Burn) and follow the path up through very tall bracken. At this point there are frequent waymarks to take the path out onto the open hillside.

However, waymarks suffer from the attention of sheep using them as scratching posts and so uprooting them from the shallow soil. Sometimes they are replaced with the direction arrows pointing in the

Salters Road

wrong direction. If in doubt about the path, climb gently in a south-westerly direction across the heathery waste until the view ahead opens up (Shank Burn should still be on your left). Head for the dip between the low, rounded Little Dod on the left (with the cairn on the summit of Hogdon Law visible beyond) and the lower slopes of Shill Moor to the right.

When the view opens up even further you will find the path still heading south-west towards a black cattle shelter with a planting of pines on the saddle of Cushat Law beyond. It soon comes to the junction with Salters Road (**B**) where the path carries straight on following a blue (bridleway) waymark. The black cattle shelter is now on the left.

Salters Road took its name from its regular use by salt traders who brought the precious commodity by this route from the salt-pans on the coast. Meat could only be preserved in bygone days by smoking or salting, so it was vital if folk were to have food other than grain in the winter. Livestock also needed salt-licks to keep healthy, and of course, Salters Road was also busy with drovers and their flocks and herds. The route was used too by whisky smugglers who carted the liquor from illicit stills hidden in remote valleys to customers in the lowland villages and towns.

The initial climb on the road is steepish but it soon levels out in a broad valley. After a gate the view westwards opens up with Bleakhope far below. The rough path follows the Hope Sike: there is quite a drop on the left but this is a very enjoyable part of the walk.

Anyone feeling fatigued at this point (**C**) could escape the rest of the walk by returning to Alnhammoor by the bridleway which follows the valley of the Breamish River. Otherwise, at Low Bleakhope turn left onto the farm road to follow the stream upriver. Pass through a series of gates at High

Bleakhope and follow the track past small areas of woodland. Quite often there is a heron fishing in the Breamish here. It seems that they invariably fly further on along the way the walker is travelling so that they are disturbed again and again, never daring to fly back past the intruder.

After another larger clump of trees (**D**), this time deciduous, climb up by the fence (taking care over wet ground) to a gate at the top. Keep on climbing to reach the top of High Cantle (**E**) where there is a mini-cairn and a stupendous view in every direction.

Cross the fence so that the one running north-east is on the left and head across the heather towards Rig Cairn whose summit can be seen ahead below that of Great Standrop.

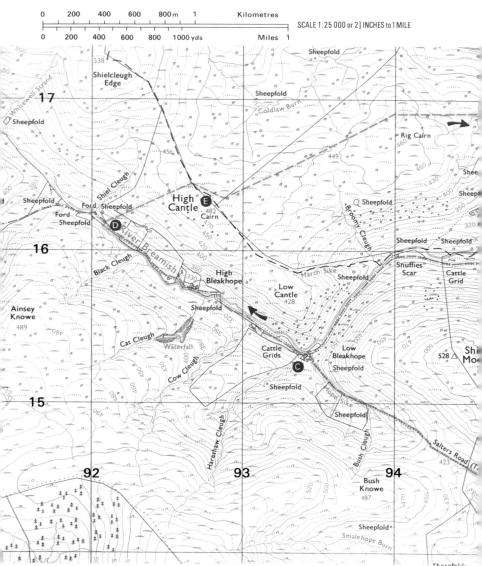

SCALE 1:25 000 or 2½ INCHES to 1 MILE

There should be twin rocky hummocks on the left. There is no trace of the right of way on the ground. Take care here, it is no place to break, or even twist, an ankle.

From Rig Cairn the view eastwards is revealed. Head in this direction, using paths made by the vehicles of shooters where possible. At first make for the plantation to the left of the conical Ritto Hill and then, when you can see it, for the gateway where three fences meet. You now follow a blue waymark which leads to a decent track going to Linhope Wood. A path to the left climbs to the waterfall (Linhope Spout) but the final part of our route bears right to reach Linhope itself, from where the road descends to Hartside.

The River Breamish near Hartside

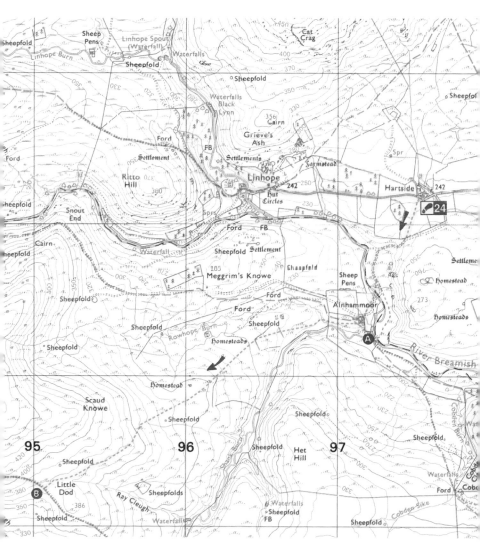

25 Craster, Howick and Longhoughton

Start:	Craster
Distance:	8 miles (12.75 km) Shorter version 4½ miles (7.25 km)
Approximate time:	4 hours (2 hours for shorter version)
Parking:	National Trust car park at Craster
Refreshments:	Pubs and cafés at Craster and at Longhoughton
Ordnance Survey maps:	Landranger 81 (Alnwick & Morpeth), and Pathfinder 477, NU 21/22 (Embleton and Alnmouth)

General description *Most people immediately head for Dunstanburgh Castle to the north of Craster (see Walk 6); this route provides a less-trodden alternative. Although the cliffs are low the seascape is never dull and on a rough day may be spectacular. There are several beaches suitable for picnicking. For the most part the return is by quiet lanes and field paths. A shorter version of the walk is suggested.*

Leave the car park by the footpath which goes towards the harbour parallel to the road, which is a little distance below. However, do not bear to the left past the tearoom towards the harbour but carry straight on, and at the road bear right following a footpath sign to Howick (there is a beguiling glimpse of the Jolly Fisherman pub in front of you before you turn to the right).

The path goes behind houses, bungalows and then a school, formerly an outdoor centre but now disused. At this point there are fields on the right and just beyond the school there is a footpath junction: take the left fork, walking towards the sea, to join with a path (**A**) near the edge of the cliff going south. This is good walking on springy turf, the waves beat on a rocky platform below. Note the jointing of the rock, typical of the Whin Sill extrusion. Behind, Dunstanburgh is in view as far as Cullernose Point, then the intriguing gothic silhouette of a house on the shore at Howick gives interest to the view ahead. Note the contortion of the strata near Swine Den; the path is narrow here, close to the cliff edge. On the right the triangulation pillar on the top of Hips Heugh is clearly visible.

The footpath bears to the left just before the road and there is a slightly prickly interlude as it passes through undergrowth between the sea and the road. However, this is brief and it soon regains its position on the open top of the cliff. The sinister house seen ahead for some time turns out to be ancient. Originally a fisherman's house, its masonry has been honeycombed by centuries of weathering.

Just beyond this, cliff erosion has forced the path away from the sea (**B**). However, the old path is still walkable (and a right of way) for a quarter of a mile and this leads to a delightful picnic spot — the beach at Rumbling Kern — where an underwater passage has been eroded to create a large pool separated from the ocean which, on a rough day, looks like a natural jacuzzi. Note the inscription on the rock here: 'Ye Howick Camp', which flourished between 1902 and 1905.

Return from this delectable spot to take the lane which leads around Sea Houses Farm.

*For the shorter walk, keep straight on down the road to reach the lodge of Howick Hall (**F**), then follow the route after (**F**) on page 66.*

Turn left at the end of the short, green lane and continue southwards after the farm, down a track which may only be used by pedestrians or disabled motorists. This field track soon reaches the seaside again at Howick Burn Mouth (**C**). Here a graceful concrete footbridge arches over the little stream. Once you have climbed to the top of the hill, on the far side you will notice a change in the coastal scenery: the clifftop is lower and there are no rocks. When you come to a made-up road on the right (**D**) (there is no longer a telephone box here) take it to reach Longhoughton.

The quiet lane reaches the village by the church. Turn left for a few yards to visit it, otherwise make a right turn at the village street, which, as the name implies, is lengthy. Pass the NAAFI stores on the right (where a tearoom is open during the week) and the Burnside Inn on the left.

At the end of the village, where the road bends sharply left, take the footpath on the right (**E**) threading through the trees. After 200 yards (183 m) turn left through a gate and follow the path on a broad headland between two crops towards a clump of trees. The path continues on the edge of the next field along another wide path. When you come to a lane turn right and follow it through beautiful woodland, crossing a road bridge over the Howick Burn and then passing beneath another bridge which takes an estate footpath over the road.

The road bends sharply to the right at the gatelodge to Howick Hall where the shorter

Craster harbour

route joins up (**F**). Keep straight on here — the footpath is to the right of the gatelodge. The hall is the home of Lord Howick, a descendant of the second Earl Grey of Reform Bill fame who lived here from 1801 until 1845. The gardens are open to the public and are at their best in spring and early summer.

Beginning as a track, the right of way soon becomes a field path following the edge of the woods. The other side of Hips Heugh can now be seen on the right, a rocky crag screened by Scots pines. On the left there is a delightful cricket ground overlooked by a house optimistically called Peep O'Sea. At the end of the woods go through the gate and walk across a broad meadow to a stile.

Over this, skirt Hips Heugh (still on the right) to reach a footpath junction (**G**) where a decision has to be made between two paths. That to the right returns to Craster via Howick Scar, which gives lovely views over the village to the castle. However it means retracing steps to make a backyard entrance to Craster.

The route to the left is preferable, using a field path to Craster South Farm. Cross the road to a kissing-gate which leads to a path through a meadow towards the cliff-face of the quarry, half-screened by trees. At the corner of this meadow close to the trees there is a gate onto a lovely woodland path which leads directly into the car park at Craster.

26 High and Low Force

Start: Bowlees Visitor Centre, near Middleton-in-Teesdale

Distance: 8 ½ miles (13.5 km)

Approximate time: 4 ½ hours

Parking: Car park at the visitor centre on the eastern side of Bow Lee Beck

Refreshments: None on the route but a pub at Langdon Beck

Ordnance Survey maps: Landrangers 91 (Appleby-in-Westmorland) and 92 (Barnard Castle), Outdoor Leisure 31 (Teesdale)

General description *The path by the River Tees upstream from Low to High Force is one of the best known footpaths in the north. This is understandable, for it not only provides the best viewpoint for one of the most spectacular British waterfalls but is also a superb riverside walk in itself. The return is on little-used paths and byways along the north side of the valley and is hardly less enjoyable. If a more taxing route is needed this can be combined with Walk 14 to take in another famous cascade — Cauldron Snout. This would cover a distance of about 17 miles (27 km).*

Refer to map overleaf.

From Bowlees car park cross the bridge to the visitor centre (which contains an exhibition illustrating the natural and human history of the area). From here go down the short lane to reach the main road and cross it to a footpath opposite the telephone box. Holwick Lodge is the large house on the other side of the valley. The footpath leads across fields to woods and then descends to Wynch Bridge (**A**), a lovely suspension bridge spanning a ravine just below the cataract of Low Force. This series of falls is more beautiful than High Force and offers photographers the opportunity of a wider range of viewpoints.

Cross the bridge and turn right to follow the river upstream past the waterfalls. Try to avoid damaging the grassy path which is assaulted by many thousands of feet each summer. It is reseeded in autumn so be careful of these bare patches. Dippers are amongst the species of birds which get their living on this stretch of the Tees.

Low Force, Teesdale

After the bridge which takes a track up to Holwick Head House climb up a reconstituted path to reach the gate into Upper Teesdale Nature Reserve. A good path threads past enormous juniper bushes which resemble the shape of Irish yews (this is the most extensive juniper wood in England). Take the path which forks to the right to view High Force. Most people see the magnificent fall from the opposite side but this spot shows it better in a setting of wild hills. With a drop of 70 feet (24 m) it is England's grandest waterfall.

Continuing westwards on the Tees-side path, the scenery is marred by the large quarry on the north side of the river. Red flags give warning of blasting. Looking away from the quarry there is a lovely waterfall on the left (Bleabeck Force) as a stream tumbles down from Whiteholm Bank. There are footbridges over a couple of sizeable streams and stepping stones over a third before the path is led up a boggy hillside (Bracken Rigg) by a causeway of planks. Near the top there

is a good view on the right over the valley to the white cottages of Forest-in-Teesdale.

There is a Pennine Way signpost a little further on (**B**). A route to Cauldron Snout (over Thistle Green to Birkdale) looks inviting on the left. However, our path is to the right, descending over rough rock to Cronkley Farm. Go through the gate with the acorn emblem of the Pennine Way on it and follow the wall on the right past the farm. Walk down the farm track to the river and cross the bridge. Turn left (**C**) onto a riverside path through a meadow. Opposite Wheysike House on the other side of the Tees the narrow path runs under a low cliff close to the river over rocks which are slippery when wet. The Pennine Way leaves our route at Saur Hill Bridge where we turn right following the sign along the track towards the Youth Hostel.

Cross straight over the road and climb up the track to East Underhurth. Go through the gate into the farmyard (**D**) and turn right, passing through another gate towards the

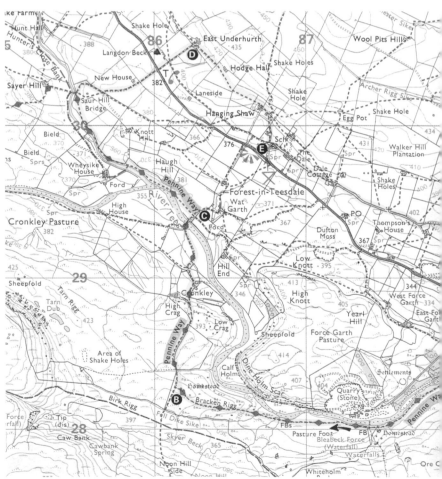

next farm, Hodge Hall. This is a lovely building characteristic of Upper Teesdale with a cattle byre at the end. Cross the field in front of the farm diagonally to a ladder over the wall in its lower right corner. Cross the next field to the farmyard of Hanging Shaw. After the two houses here follow the farm drive down towards the main road. Before you reach it turn left at the school (**E**).

After the cottage called 'The Dale' it looks as though you're walking to a dead-end of undergrowth. Persevere to a stile at the end of this and climb it into a sunken lane running beside the wall on the right: this was once the main road. Pass in front of Dale Cottage to join a made-up road. There is an Ebenezer Methodist chapel on the left dating from 1880. Carry straight on when the road bears right to a farm. There are still traces of an ancient trackway here with a slight embankment on the left (the wall is on the right). Go through a black gate — there is a cottage on the right, East Moor Riggs — and then two more gates to head for the farmhouse with the black shed below (the one on the right, not a similar one — Birch Bush — further up on the left). Go to the left of the former cottage, which is Birch Rigg, to reach the road and turn right.

After half a mile (0.75 km) fork left off this road (**F**) to Dirt Pitt — a misnomer for a charming spot with its stream, waterfall, and lovely cottage sporting a porch packed full of geraniums. The name is actually a corruption of Deer Peth, a reference to an ancient hunting forest. Beyond here the lane

High Force

becomes a track, dipping down to another stream. This is glorious countryside with views through 360 degrees. Ash Hill is passed on the right and the woods surrounding Bowlees come into view. The final part of the walk is through delightful meadowland (please remember to shut the gates), dipping down to reach the visitor centre which was our starting point.

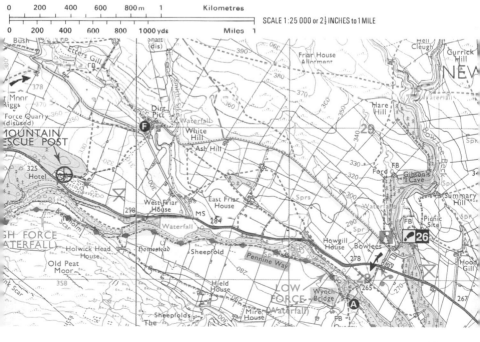

0   200   400   600   800 m   1   Kilometres

0   200   400   600   800   1000 yds   Miles   1

SCALE 1:25 000 or 2½ INCHES to 1 MILE

27 Crosthwaite Common, Rake Gill and Holwick

Start:	Middleton-in-Teesdale
Distance:	9½ miles (15.25 km)
Approximate time:	4½ hours
Parking:	Middleton-in-Teesdale (Hill Terrace is the most convenient)
Refreshments:	Pubs and cafés at Middleton, Strathmore Arms at Holwick (children welcome)
Ordnance Survey maps:	Landrangers 91 (Appleby-in-Westmorland) and 92 (Barnard Castle), Outdoor Leisure 31 (Teesdale)

General description *The triangular shape of this route divides, predictably, into three sections. The outward stretch is along the Pennine Way out of Middleton, good walking across pastures with excellent views over Teesdale and then Lunedale, with its man-made lakes. Then the path turns off to the north-west on a bridleway (sometimes quite difficult to follow on the ground) over grouse moors to reach Holwick. From here the way back is straightforward, following the riverside path (the Pennine Way again) by the River Tees. It would be as well to bring a compass on this walk.*

Refer to map on pages 72 and 73.

Cross the bridge at Middleton-in-Teesdale following the road to Brough and Scotch Corner. Pass the livestock mart and where the Holwick road goes off the main road to the right take this turn and immediately look for a bridleway on the left (**A**). Go through the gate to walk up the hill on this track. The view of the small town in its lovely valley is outstanding and improves as you get higher.

After a green gate bear to the right away from the wall, heading towards a flat-topped hill. As you climb there is a distinctive clump of trees on top of the hill to your left which marks the site of Kirkcarrion, a burial ground of the Bronze Age. You will be walking up a path on the left side of a gully heading towards a gate. After the gate (**B**) fork to the right making for the flat-topped hill. The path skirts to the left of its summit: there is a helpful cairn to guide the way.

Go through the gate in the corner of the pasture at the top. There is a yellow waymark on the next gate: turn right after this to another gate which has distinctive white-painted steps taking the path over the wall to its left. Now follow the path towards a post bearing a white flash which stands by a small cairn. From here the view opens up over Lunedale and the reservoirs. Follow the yellow waymark, bearing right towards Selset Reservoir.

Beyond the next gate a grassy track leads past a cattle byre. Cross a stone stile by a gate and head for the farm in the distance ahead (Cornset). After another gate the path descends to a track which goes through a gateway (**C**) with a yellow waymark. Go down this track for 50 yards (46 m) and then bear off it to the right through a gateway heading for Wythes Hill Farm. Cross a stream by stepping stones and continue down to ford the Carl Beck. Just before the farm, where the track bears left (**D**), go through a gate on the right (a figure 8 is painted on the stone gatepost).

Turn left to follow the wall on the left. The Carl Beck is now on the right. After a gate, the wall you have been following bears off to the left. Here the track is vague but by walking in the same direction (with Cornset ahead, but to the right, two fields distant) you will approach another wall on the right-hand side. There should be a small stream on the left where the track passes through a red gate onto what looks like the open moor. However, there is still another gate ahead: you reach this by walking with the fence to the right.

Now keep Cornset's boundary wall to the right as the path winds along on the left bank of Merry Gill which it eventually crosses (**E**), close to a skeletal shed. From here make for stonework ruins and then follow a winding track into the heathery wastes. It climbs steeply at first, heading north-west, but then levels out. A stone wall comes into view on the left and the path drops down into Rake Gill (**F**), a concealed valley with shooting butts, a shelter, and even a privy.

From the shelter bear left to climb out of the gill. Go through the gate where the track ends and follow the path which passes to the right of a further flat-topped hill. Suddenly, Teesdale is revealed below. This is a spectacular surprise.

Go through a red gate and begin to descend on a reasonably clear, but soggy, path. This is Crooks o' Green Fell: to the left are rocky crags. When you see a wall ahead strike off to the right keeping the wall to the left. You should be close to the wall to cross a stream (Easter Beck): after this there is something of a path leading to a gate at the bottom (**G**).

Go through the gate and keep on the

distinct path which follows a line bisecting the angle between the wall (on the right) and the fence (left). Cross the Rowton Beck and then head for a white-painted stile below. From here the route is very clearly marked by white posts. It passes a sheepfold and short stretch of high stone walling to reach another white stile. Bear right here following the white arrow on the stile, passing cairns, to enter a steep and narrow valley which seems to be leading over the crest of the crag (although this looks like a quarry, in fact it is a natural feature). However there is a well-concealed stile here. One might be tempted to think that this is a subterfuge for getting rid of ramblers, but there is a way down, though it is a steep scramble, with the stream to the left. At the bottom cross the stream and climb the steep bank to turn right (**H**) onto the track to Holwick.

The pub in Holwick, the Strathmore Arms, lies 400 yards (366 m) beyond the point in the village where a path to the left, about 100 yards (91 m) past the telephone box, takes the route down to the River Tees and then onward into Middleton. Thoughtfully, a stile is placed to avoid the morass at the end of the first field. There is a white-painted stile at the bottom of the next one, but the path does not cross this: instead it goes through one in the wall on the right to reach the riverbank by a footbridge. Do not cross this but turn right, following the riverside path eastwards.

There seems to be an endless succession of stiles on this path, which follows the river's course for much of the way through the meadows. It cuts across three of the more extreme meanders as it approaches Middleton and for a short distance follows a sunken lane which has a very ancient feel to it. The path finally leaves the riverside to join a farm track leading past the livestock mart to reach the main road. Turn left here to cross the bridge and return to Middleton.

Middleton-in-Teesdale

28 Around The Cheviot from Harthope Valley

Start:	The Harthope Valley before Langleeford
Distance:	12 miles (19 km)
Approximate time:	6½ hours
Parking:	Off the road before Langleeford
Refreshments:	None
Ordnance Survey maps:	Landrangers 74 (Kelso) and 75 (Berwick-upon-Tweed), Pathfinders 475, NT 82/92 (The Cheviot Hills North) and 487, NT 81/91 (The Cheviot Hills Central)

General description *Gradients are rarely the problem in the Cheviots, the main cause of fatigue is likely to be the incessant wind, so choose a day of soft breezes and good visibility for this walk. Once on the border ridge, and if you still have the energy, it is comparatively easy to visit the summit of The Cheviot — allow an extra hour. Although there is about ½ mile (0.75 km) of duckboarding after Auchope Cairn, there is still a lot of boggy ground after this and it is hard to escape without at least one boot filled with peaty fluid. The return down to the Harthope Valley is over rough ground, and once the side of the stream is reached the path is little better than a sheep track.*

Refer to map on pages 76 and 77.

Just before the wall which marks the boundary of the Langleeford property there is a narrow bridleway leaving the road to the right waymarked to Broadstruther and Goldscleugh. The path follows the right bank of the Hawsen Burn, keeping fairly well up on the side of the valley but low enough to pass by a stell (circular sheepfold) after the bridleway to Anstruther has gone off to the right. Looking back across the Harthope Valley, the summits of Housey and Langlee Crags are distinctive landmarks which are a welcome sight on the return leg of the route. They are tors, akin to those on Dartmoor, residues of hard volcanic rocks which forced their way to the surface from the earth's core 380 million years ago.

Beyond the sheepfold the lower slopes of the valley of the Hawsen Burn are precipitous and the faint path winds westwards above them eventually arriving at a fence. Make for the gate in it (**A**) and pass through it to begin descending into the lovely valley ahead, heading for the bottom of the plantation on the right. The massive bulk of The Cheviot is on the left.

Cross a stile bearing a waymark at a gate near the lower end of the plantation into a broad, level windbreak. Follow the path to the western end of the wood: there is a thicket of tall, fragrant broom growing here. Go through this to a gate and then follow along the top of the plantation (watch out for adders on this path) to a gateway at the end. Beyond this there is a faint path along the flank of the valley which is soon joined by another path which has followed the valley below the wood.

Keep on the right side of the stream towards Goldscleugh to join with a track which goes through the 'inbye' land (the sheltered, relatively fertile enclosures of the valley bottom close to the farm). Cross the ford (**B**) (or the footbridge a little way upstream) and climb the track the short distance to the gate. After this turn right to pass in front of the farmhouse. Cross another stream and keep outside the walls of the farmyard to pass to the right of a black corrugated-metal building. Make for the gateway ahead, keeping below the slope with the birch trees. Turn left onto the road.

A pleasant stretch follows on an even surface. There are views of the ravine below Dunsdale Crag. A footpath leaves the road on the left: take this to cut off a corner towards the white-painted cottage of Dunsdale. Before the building, look to the left up the stream. This is the Bizzle Burn which comes down from the top of The Cheviot through a steep ravine. Pass through the yard at Dunsdale to a gate by a black shed. Go through this and two more gates to reach the edge of a plantation. Turn left to follow its edge — this is excellent walking on a grassy path. As the way begins to drop towards Mounthooly the way ahead to the ridge looks forbidding. When the trees end there is a fine view of The Schill. Pass to the right side of the fence but continue to follow it. Cross the Breydon Burn and then go through the gate close to the stell to drop down to cross College Burn. There is a sort of rickety footbridge incorporated into the fence here. Having crossed the Burn head up to the trees and turn left onto a clear path (**C**).

This is easy to follow as far as Smeddon Sike(**D**): before the stell here make for the topmost plantation. Turn left again here to follow the fence, and then at the end of the somewhat stunted pines bear slightly to the right to begin the climb over rough ground to Red Cribs. The latter is a gash in the hillside which should be passed on its right (north-west) side. The border fence is soon visible at the crest of the climb. Turn left to follow the Pennine Way eastwards (E).

The mountain refuge hut is situated close to this point before the next challenge — the long climb up to Auchope Cairn. The refuge offers shelter from the weather and a superb view of the surrounding heights. The Hen Hole, best seen from Auchope Cairn, is the awesome chasm from where music of magical sweetness is said to emanate, enticing the unwary to fall to its rocky depths. Sunshine never reaches these depths and snow is said to linger on midsummer day.

The cairn itself (F) stands at a height of 2,418 feet (737 m), just 256 feet (78 m) less than The Cheviot summit, and is surrounded by a sea of shattered rock. It is certainly a better viewpoint, one of the finest in England — by using binoculars on a clear day you are supposed to be able to identify the shape of Lochnagar, near Balmoral on Deeside, over 100 miles (160 km) distant.

From Auchope Cairn the route continues south-eastwards along the Pennine Way over about ½ mile (0.75 km) of duckboarding. At the end of this there is a signpost. Bear left to follow the very boggy footpath towards Cheviot summit. A line of old fencing posts marks the route which cuts across boggy ground to the north of the fence. When it meets with the fence again follow it to Scotsman's Cairn (G). If you wish to visit the summit of The Cheviot, continue to follow the fence over boggy, though level, ground. This diversion will take at least an hour so make sure that you have time and energy enough to undertake it.

If you do not intend to make this diversion, or are returning from having made it, cross the fence by the stile and begin a descent over difficult ground towards the Harthope Valley. The direction is south-east, that is at right angles to the fence behind the cairn. After a few paces in this direction the head of the Harthope Valley is obvious below. Take great care in descending over the tussocky grass: it would be unwise to sprain an ankle here. The water flowing from the innumerable springs on this slope has a delicious sweetness and purity.

At the bottom a very faint path follows the embryonic stream, crossing from side to side at first. After a while it settles for its left bank and the stream grows from a trickle to a splash. The path becomes better defined as well. Harthope Linn is a beautiful waterfall contained in a shady dell — an ideal place for a picnic.

Pass to the right of the sheep-pens at Langleeford Hope. Ford the stream and pass behind the house to join the track leading down the valley. From here the walking is comparatively restful, but also very pretty with Housey Crag and the mesa-like Langlee Crag prominent landmarks. After Langleeford the road is made-up and runs by the inbye land of the farm. It soon reaches the Hawsen Burn and the starting point of the walk.

The Cheviot from above Goldscleugh

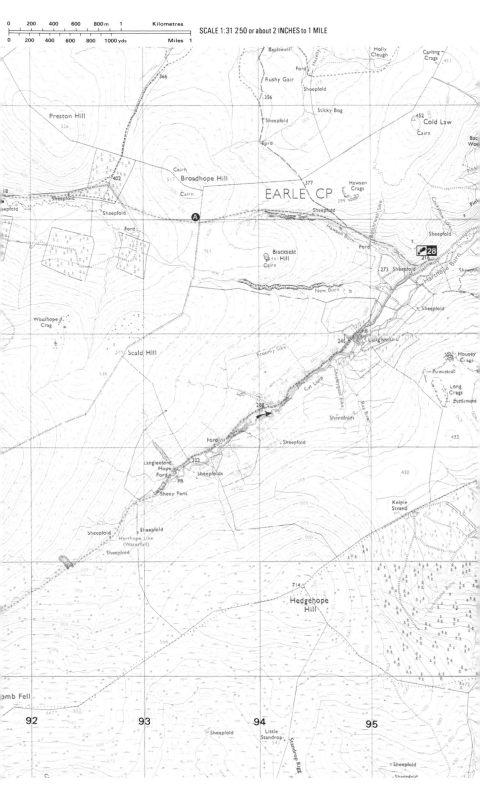

SCALE 1:31 250 or about 2 INCHES to 1 MILE

Useful organisations

The Countryside Commission,
John Dower House, Crescent Place,
Cheltenham, Gloucestershire GL50 3RA.
Tel: 0242 521381

The National Trust,
36 Queen Anne's Gate, London SW1H 9AS.
Tel: 071 222 9251
(Northumbria Regional Office, Scots' Gap,
Morpeth, Northumberland NE61 4EG.
Tel: 067 074 691)

Council for National Parks,
246 Lavender Hill, London SW11 1LJ.
Tel: 071 924 4077

Northumberland National Park,
Eastburn, South Park, Hexham, Northumberland
NE46 1BS. Tel: 0434 605555.

National Park Authority Information Centres can
be found at:
Once Brewed (Tel: 0434 344396)
Ingram (Tel: 0665 78248)
Rothbury (Tel: 0669 20887)

Northumbria Tourist Board,
Aykley Heads, Durham DH1 5UX.
Tel: 091 384 6905

Northumbrian Water,
Kielder Water Tower Knowe Visitor Centre,
Falstone, Northumberland. Tel: 0434 240398

The Ramblers' Association,
1/5 Wandsworth Road, London SW8 2XX.
Tel: 071 582 6878

The Forestry Commission,
Information Branch, 231 Corstorphine Road,
Edinburgh EH12 7AT. Tel: 031 334 0303

The Youth Hostels Association,
Trevelyan House, 8 St Stephen's Hill, St Albans,
Hertfordshire AL1 2DY. Tel: 0727 855215

The Long Distance Walkers' Association,
7 Ford Drive, Yarnfield, Stone,
Staffordshire ST15 0RP.

The Council for the Protection of Rural England,
Warwick House, 25 Buckingham Palace Road,
London SW1W 0PP. Tel: 071 976 6433.

Ordnance Survey,
Romsey Road, Maybush, Southampton
SO9 4DH. Tel: 0703 792763/4/5 or 792792

Ordnance Survey maps of Northumbria

Northumbria is covered by Ordnance Survey
1:50 000 scale (1¼ inches to 1 mile) Landranger
map sheets 74, 75, 80, 81, 86, 87, 88, 91 and 92.
These all-purpose maps are packed with
information to help you explore the area.
Viewpoints, picnic sites, places of interest, caravan
and camping sites are shown, as well as public
rights of way information such as footpaths and
bridleways.

To examine Northumbria in more detail and
especially if you are planning walks, Ordnance
Survey Pathfinder maps at 1:25 000 (2½ inches to 1
mile) scale are ideal. Maps covering this area are:

435 (NT 45/55)	473 (NT 42/52)
436 (NT 65/75)	474 (NT 62/72)
437 (NT 85)	475 (NT 82/92)
438 (NT 95/NU 05)	476 (NU 02/12)
449 (NT 44/54)	477 (NU 21/22)
450 (NT 64/74)	485 (NT 41/51)
451 (NT 84/94)	486 (NT 61/71)
452 (NU 04/14)	487 (NT 81/91)
461 (NT 43/53)	488 (NU 01/11)
462 (NT 63/73)	497 (NT 40/50)
463 (NT 83/93)	498 (NT 60/70)
464 (NU 03)	499 (NT 80/90)
465 (NU 13/23)	500 (NU 00/10)

501 (NU 20)		550 (NZ 45/46)
508 (NY 49/59)		558 (NY 45/55)
509 (NY 69/79)		559 (NY 65/75)
510 (NY 89/99)		560 (NY 85/95)
511 (NZ 09/19)		561 (NZ 05/15)
512 (NZ 29)		562 (NZ 25/35)
520 (NY 48/58)		568 (NY 44/54)
522 (NY 88/98)		569 (NY 64/74)
523 (NZ 08/18)		570 (NY 84/94)
524 (NZ 28/38)		571 (NZ 04/14)
532 (NY 47/57)		572 (NZ 24/34)
533 (NY 67/77)		573 (NZ 44)
534 (NY 87/97)		577 (NY 43/53)
535 (NZ 07/17)		578 (NY 62/63)
536 (NZ 27/37)		580 (NZ 12/13)
545 (NY 46/56)		581 (NZ 23/33)
546 (NY 66/76)		582 (NZ 43/53)
547 (NY 86/96)		590 (NZ 22/32)
548 (NZ 06/16)		591 (NZ 42/52)
549 (NZ 26/36)		592 (NZ 62/72)

Explorer map 1 (Kielder Water) and Outdoor
Leisure map 31 (Teesdale) are also at 1:25 000 scale
(2½ inches to 1 mile).

Tourists will also find the Touring Map and Guide
14, of Northumbria, useful as it provides lots of
information on where to go and what to see.

To get to Northumbria, use the Ordnance Survey
Routemaster map number 4 (Central Scotland and
Northumberland) at 1:250 000 (1 inch to 4 miles)
scale.

Ordnance Survey maps and guides are available
from most booksellers, stationers and newsagents.

Index